W9-AXZ-355

INSTRUCTOR'S MANUAL

CASES IN FINANCIAL REPORTING

An Integrated Approach with an Emphasis on Earnings Quality and Persistence

Third Edition

D. Eric Hirst

University of Texas at Austin

Mary Lea McAnally

University of Texas at Austin

Prentice Hall

Upper Saddle River, New Jersey 07458

Acquisitions editor: Deborah Hoffman
Associate editor: Kathryn Sheehan
Production editor: Theresa Festa
Manufacturer: Technical Communication Services

ISBN 0-13-084018-1
10 9 8 7 6 5 4 3 2 1

CASES IN FINANCIAL REPORTING
AN INTEGRATED APPROACH
WITH AN EMPHASIS ON EARNINGS QUALITY AND PERSISTENCE

CONTENTS

Cases are listed in CONCEPTUAL *order. They are found in* ALPHABETICAL *order.*

BECOMING FAMILIAR WITH FINANCIAL REPORTING
Basics, Tools, and the Persistence of Earnings

EVALUATING FINANCIAL REPORTING DISCLOSURES
Balance Sheet Components and Issues in the Quality of Earnings

Assets
L.A. Gear, Inc.—Cash and Balance Sheet Issues
Analog Devices, Inc.—Revenue Recognition
The Warnaco Group Inc.—Accounts Receivable
Lands' End, Inc.—Inventory
Callaway Golf Company—Manufacturing Inventory
Frederick's of Hollywood—Property & Equipment
Chambers Development Co. Inc.—Capitalizing Costs
Merck & Co., Inc.—Research & Development
eBay—Acquired in-Process Research and Development
America Online, Inc.—Deferred Costs

Liabilities
E.I. du Pont de Nemours—Environmental Matters
Maytag Corporation—Warranties & Deferred Taxes
Eastman Kodak and Polaroid—Contingencies
Bally Entertainment Corporation—Long-Term Debt
The Home Depot—Long Term Debt
AMR Corporation—Leases
The Robert Mondavi Corporation—Deferred Taxes
Bethlehem Steel—Pension Obligations
Black Clawson—Other Post-Employment Benefits

Owners' Equity
The Dow Chemical Company—Treasury Stock

Intercorporate Investments
Wachovia—Marketable Securities
BCE Inc.—Investments in Other Companies
The Seagram Company—Investments in Common Stock

Financial Statement Analysis
Boston Beer & Lion Brewery—Financial Statement Analysis

CASES IN FINANCIAL REPORTING
AN INTEGRATED APPROACH
WITH AN EMPHASIS ON EARNINGS QUALITY AND PERSISTENCE

PREFACE

This book is a collection of financial accounting cases designed to help students become financial statement users. Each case contains financial statement information (a balance sheet, income statement, statement of cash flow and/or footnotes) and a number of topical questions. Students use the financial statement information to infer and interpret the economic events underlying the numbers.

We use the materials with M.B.A. students in their required Financial Accounting class and in executive education programs. However, the intended audience for the material also includes undergraduate students at the introductory level, undergraduate and M.B.A. intermediate students, as well as students in financial statement analysis classes.

NEW IN THE 3RD EDITION

In keeping with the contemporary flavor of the first two editions, approximately one-third of the cases have been either updated to more recent financial statements or are completely new. We have reduced the total number of cases, eliminating ones covering more technical issues and combining others to reduce redundancies. All cases have been reviewed with an eye to improving their clarity.

In this edition, the cases are found alphabetically by company name. To get a feel for the scope of the cases as a whole, we refer you to the table of contents. There, the cases are presented in a conceptual order—the order we use them at the McCombs School of Business at the University of Texas at Austin.

THE 'CPA' APPROACH—CONCEPTS, PROCESS, AND ANALYSIS

As in the second edition, the questions are organized in "C.P.A." order.

Concepts   The typical case begins with a set of conceptual questions. As we introduce each topic area, we want to ensure that students are familiar with the vocabulary and the broader concepts before moving into the specific application to the case-corporation. These general questions focus each case on its topic area. For example, the Maytag case on warranties begins with the conceptual questions "from the consumer's standpoint, what is a warranty?" and "from Maytag's standpoint, what is a warranty?" Here too, we require students to retrieve specific information from the financial statements but not to manipulate it. For example, the Deere case on marketable securities asks "what balance did the company report on its balance sheet for trading securities?" Because the concept questions call for factual responses, lower-level skills are required. Students' confidence increases with these opening questions.

Process   Before students become sophisticated consumers of accounting information they need an understanding of the accounting process and the basics of financial statement preparation. Thus, the second set of questions in each case focuses on the process. Process questions require students to manipulate financial statement information via calculations, journal entries, and T-accounts. It is at this point that many textbook exercises end. However, we believe that the accounting process is not the end but the means by which students build a firm understanding of how financial accounting works the way it does.

Analysis   With a strong understanding of the concepts and a solid knowledge of the accounting cycle, students are ready for higher level analytical questions. These questions have students synthesize, analyze, interpret information and formulate and defend opinions. Thus, higher-order thinking skills are required in the analysis questions.

By grouping the case questions into the C.P.A. categories, the text has broad audience. Taken alone, the Concept and Process questions are perfectly aimed at undergraduate introductory financial accounting classes. Because many M.B.A. students have taken some accounting and most have had some business experience, they are better prepared to handle the Analysis questions even at the introductory level. Several topics (e.g. pensions, OPEB, marketable securities, deferred taxes) are not typically covered in an introductory course. These can be used at the intermediate level for undergraduate and M.B.A. classes. For intermediate and financial statement analysis courses, the Concept questions can be used to start the class discussion each day. Taking up these questions first ensures that the students are on common ground before they go on to tackle the more challenging Analysis questions. The full set of financial statements included with each case affords the class instructor the opportunity to expand the analytical questions or to explore issues the Analysis questions do not touch upon.

HOW TO USE THESE MATERIALS

These cases are designed to be used in conjunction with an introductory, intermediate, or financial statement analysis textbook. The order in which material is presented by an instructor does not affect the relevance of the cases. Each case stands alone and while some cases naturally precede others, there is no prescribed order.

Although the cases are companion to a text they are much more than supplementary material. Since 1991, these materials have been used as the primary basis for the class meetings in the semester-long introductory financial accounting class at the University of Texas at Austin. The cases provide the learning ground for students (who are expected to prepare the questions before class). For the most part, the questions, when handled by the students, raise most of the salient points in each topic area. Short (10-15 minute) lectures have *occasionally* been included to supplement the real world applications provided by the case material.

The table of contents reflects the order in which we use the cases in our course at the McCombs School of Business at the University of Texas at Austin. We have organized our course around two main themes—earnings persistence and the quality of earnings. The first third of the course is spent learning the basic framework of financial reporting, acquiring skills in basic financial statement preparation, and in understanding how financial statements aid in the investment decision process. In achieving the latter, we emphasize how financial statements classify items and how such classifications are important in the prediction of the nature, uncertainty, and timing of future cash flows. Thus, we introduce the notion of earnings *persistence* and how it affects firm valuation. The remainder of the course explores the accounting issues for the major financial statement line items. We place particular emphasis on the latitude and judgment management has in arriving at the reported numbers and the economic consequences of their choices. This introduces the notion of the *quality* of earnings. The cases included here help students acquire the skills necessary to identify quality of earnings issues and learn how to deal with them (for example, by restating the financials under different assumptions or accounting methods).

Not all the cases are used over the course of the semester. For each class meeting, one case is assigned as the main case. Students have, in the past, handed in their responses to the main case *before it is discussed in class*. This serves three purposes. First, it ensures that students are ready to take-up the material during the class period. Second, it provides evidence of students' progress or need for assistance and can be used for evaluation purposes. Third, and most importantly, it puts the onus for learning the material on the student. Often, the case affords them their initial formal encounter with accounting concepts. This means that the students teach themselves the material. Their learning becomes *active*. The alternative is for students to come to class and have an instructor teach the material to them. This makes their learning *passive*. Psychology studies have shown that active learning leads to greater retention and deeper comprehension.

Students can be assigned to small study groups of 5 to 7 students to foster a team-approach to learning. Group work can be actively encouraged outside the classroom by allowing group responses to the main case or by assigning to study-groups, the responsibility for initiating and managing in-class response to the main case. In-class discussions and negotiation exercises can be generated by having study-groups take opposing arguments or by assigning roles to conflicted parties in the case.

THINGS TO STRESS EARLY IN THE COURSE

These materials represent a unique collection of cases. You can motivate students by making them explicitly aware of the following attributes:

Financial Statement Use over Preparation—The preponderance of students who come into contact with financial statement information, subsequent to accounting classes, will be users rather than preparers of that information. Encourage students to think of accounting as the language of business. Stress that their future success in business depends, in part, on their ability to use accounting information to make decisions. Explain that the focus of the materials in this casebook is on financial statement use. The foray into the mechanics of financial accounting in the early cases builds an understanding of how financial statements are put together so that, later, they can be taken apart and the components "used" to make informed business decisions.

Earnings Quality and Persistence—The cases have been designed around two main themes: the quality and persistence of earnings. Introduce issues of quality and persistence early in the course. First, emphasize through discussion and in-class solution of cases, how financial statements classify items and how such classifications are important in the prediction of the timing of future cash flows. Echo the notion that earnings *persistence* affects firm valuation. Second, encourage students to critically explore the accounting issues for the major financial statement line items with a view to evaluating management discretion over accounting policies. Place particular emphasis on the latitude and judgment management has in arriving at the reported numbers. This introduces the notion of the *quality* of earnings. The final question of the first case in this book can be used to set the tone: Based on your review of the financial statements of Maytag Corp., list as many of the estimates underlying the financial statements as you can. Are any of Maytag's accounts "estimate-free"?

Financial Statement Diversity—This book comprises 39 cases covering 40 reporting entities. We believe that you will appreciate the exposure to many different companies and quickly learn that, while financial statements do not all look the same, they *can* all be understood and used.

Current Financial Statements—The cases are very current; primarily dated 1995 through 1999. This affords you the opportunity to read and use pertinent and timely financial information. Some older cases have been included because they explicate a concept particularly well or because they demonstrate an uncommon trend.

International Financial Statements—Cases cover companies from France, Japan, the U.K. and Canada as well as from the U.S. Many of the U.S. companies are major multinationals. Increased globalization of business necessitates your facility with financial statements other than those prepared in accordance with U.S. GAAP. Some international cases require you to recast the financials to U.S. GAAP. Thus, you will become a sophisticated user of financial information.

Internet Format of Corporate Reports—Many of the financial statements, MD&A, Forms 10-K and 10-Q, and other corporate information in the casebook have been retrieved from the Securities and Exchange Commission's EDGAR database. The presentation of the material has been deliberately left consistent with the on-line presentation. If you are already accessing this type of information on-line, the presentation in these cases will be familiar to you.

Learning Objectives—Cases are prefaced with a set of learning objectives. These become your learning goals as you work through the cases. The focus of each case is made clear through these objectives.

Corporate Descriptions—Each case focuses on one or two sets of financial statements. A brief description of the companies in the case is designed to remind you that accounting information is used in specific business contexts. Reported financial accounting numbers are the result of a series of complex, professional estimates and judgments. Many of these are influenced by industry practice. Correctly reading and interpreting financial information is predicated on your awareness of a company's business and industry. This fact needs to be repeated often during the semester.

Although we have made every effort to avoid errors, any that remain are solely our responsibility. Should you have any suggestions for improving this product, we would love to hear from you. We can be reached by telephone, fax, or e-mail as follows:

	Telephone	Fax	E-mail
Eric Hirst	512-471-5565	512-471-3904	Eric.Hirst@bus.utexas.edu
Mary Lea McAnally	512-471-2163	512-471-3904	MaryLea.McAnally@bus.utexas.edu

Teaching Notes:

This case has the benefit of discussing a company whose products are familiar to most students.

The process portion of the case helps students learn to prepare financial statements. Students start with the prior year's ending balances, post transactions, book several adjusting journal entries, prepare the balance sheet and income statement, and prepare closing entries. The entries are sufficiently basic that, when provided with the financial statements as a guide, students are able to answer the questions.

Combined with the Food Lion case, this case helps students gain a facility with the preparation of financial statements. It is important to stress, however, that preparation is the means to an end—reading and interpreting financial statements and analyzing accounting data with a view to understanding the economics underlying the published reports is considerably easier if students first have a working knowledge of accounting mechanics.

The analysis portion of the case has students calculate some simple ratios and interpret the trends they find. As well, question j. brings students back to the notion that financial reports have the express purpose of helping investors assess the nature and timing of future cash flows and earnings.

Abercrombie & Fitch Co.—Transactions and Financial Statements

a.

Cash and Equivalents

Beg. bal.	42,667			
(3)	800,000			
(5)	13,398	514,114	(6)	
(7)	23,785	50,000	(8)	
		908	(9)	
		151,264	(11)	
End bal.	163,564			

Accounts Receivable

Beg. bal.	1,695			
(3)	15,804	13,398	(5)	
End bal.	4,101			

Inventories

Beg. bal.	33,927	465,000	(4)	
(1)	481,918	6,853	(12a)	
End bal.	43,992			

Accounts Payable

Beg. bal.		15,968		
(6)	514,114	481,918	(1)	
		1,000	(2)	
		39,987	(9)	
End bal.		24,759		

Accrued Expenses

Beg. bal.		35,143		
		25,054	(11)	
		3,685	(12e)	
End bal.		63,882		

Income Taxes Payable

Beg. bal.		15,851		
		17,736	(11)	
End bal.		33,587		

Other Long-Term Liabilities

Beg. bal.		7,501		
		3,327	(11)	
End bal.		10,828		

Paid-in Capital

Beg. bal.		117,972		
		26,170	(11)	
End bal.		144,142		

Treasury Stock

Beg. bal.	777	
(10)	908	
End bal.	1,685	

Store Supplies

Beg. bal.	5,592	705	(12b)	
(2)	1,000			
End bal.	5,887			

Receivable from The Limited

Beg. bal.	23,785			
		23,785	(7)	
End bal.	0			

Other Current Assets

Beg. bal.	1,296	1,005	(12c)	
(11)	400			
End bal.	691			

Property & Equipment (net)

Beg. bal.	70,517			
(9)	39,987	20,946	(12d)	
End bal.	89,558			

Deferred Income Taxes

Beg. bal.	3,759			
(11)	6,978			
End bal.	10,737			

Other Assets

Beg. bal.	0	
(11)	631	
End bal.	631	

Long-Term Debt

Beg. bal.		50,000		
(8)	50,000			
End bal.		0		

Common Stock

Beg. bal.		511		
		6	(11)	
End bal.		517		

Retained Earnings (Deficit)

Beg. bal.	58,931			
		102,062	(13)	
End bal.		43,131		

Sales

Beg. bal.		0	
(13)	815,804	815,804	(3)
End bal.		0	

COGS, Occupancy, and Buying Costs

Beg. bal.	0		
(4)	465,000	471,853	(13)
(12a)	6,853		
end bal.	0		

Investment Income, net

Beg. bal.		0	
(13)	3,144	3,144	(11)
End bal.		0	

Provision for Income Taxes (Expense)

beg. bal.	0		
(11)	68,040	68,040	(13)
end bal.	0		

General, Administrative, & Store Operating Expenses

Beg. bal.	0		
(11)	150,652	176,993	(13)
(12b)	705		
(12c)	1,005		
(12d)	20,946		
(12e)	3,685		
end bal.	0		

Note: these T-accounts include the adjusting and closing entries from parts c and f. The unadjusted trial balance in part b excludes those entries. The adjusted trial balance excludes the closing entry.

b. January 30, 1999 Unadjusted Trial Balance

	Debits	Credits
Cash	163,564	
Accounts Receivable	4,101	
Inventories	50,845	
Store Supplies	6,592	
Receivable from the Limited	0	
Other Current Assets	1,696	
Property and Equipment net	110,504	
Deferred Income Taxes	10,737	
Other Assets	631	
Accounts Payable		24,759
Accrued Expenses		60,197
Income Taxes Payable		33,587
Long-Term Debt		0
Other Long-Term Liabilities		10,828
Common Stock		517
Paid-In Capital		144,142
Retained Earnings/Deficit	58,931	
Treasury Stock	1,685	
Net Sales		815,804
COGS, Occupancy, Buying Costs	465,000	
Gen., Admin., and Store Operating Expenses	150,652	
Interest Income		3,144
Provision for Income Taxes	68,040	
	1,092,978	1,092,978

c. Adjusting Journal Entries

(12a)

Dr.	Cost of Goods Sold, Occupancy, and Buying Costs	6,853*	
Cr.	Inventories		6,853
	To record physical inventory count.		

* Unadjusted balance less physical count: $50,845 - $43,992 = $6,853.

(12b)
Dr. General, Administrative, & Store Operating Expenses   705
        Store Supplies   705
    To record physical count of store supplies.

* Unadjusted balance less physical count: $6,592 – $5,887 = $705.

(12c)
Dr. General, Administrative, & Store Operating Expenses   1,005*
Cr.   Other Current assets   1,005
    To record remaining prepaid insurance.

* Unadjusted balance less unexpired premium: $1,696 – $691 = $1,005.

(12d)
Dr. General, Administrative, & Store Operating Expenses   20,946
Cr.   PPE, net   20,946
    To record depreciation.

(12d)
Dr. General, Administrative, & Store Operating Expenses   3,685
Cr.   Accrued Liabilities   3,685
    To record unpaid wages owed at year end.

d. January 30, 1999 Adjusted Trial Balance

	Debits	Credits
Cash	163,564	
Accounts Receivable	4,101	
Inventories	43,992	
Store Supplies	5,887	
Receivable from the Limited	0	
Other Current Assets	691	
P&E net	89,558	
Deferred Income Taxes	10,737	
Other Assets	631	
Accounts Payable		24,759
Accrued Expenses		63,882
Income Taxes Payable		33,587
Long-Term Debt		0
Other Long-Term Liabilities		10,828
Common Stock		517
Paid-In Capital		144,142
Retained Earnings/Deficit	58,931	
Treasury Stock	1,685	
Net Sales		815,804
COGS, Occupancy, Buying Costs	471,853	
Gen., Admin., and Store Operating Expenses	176,993	
Interest Income		3,144
Provision for Income Taxes	68,040	
	1,096,663	1,096,663

e. Fiscal 1999 Income Statement:

	1999
Sales	$815,804
Cost of Goods Sold, Occupancy and Buying Costs	(471,853)
Gross Income (Gross Margin)	343,951
General, Administrative and Store Operating Expense	(176,993)
Operating Income	166,958
Interest Income	3,144
Income Before Taxes	170,102
Provision for Income Taxes	(68,040)
Net Income	102,062

f. Closing Entries

(13)
Dr.	Sales	815,804	
Dr.	Interest Income	3,144	
Cr.	Cost of Goods Sold, Occupancy, and Buying Costs		471,853
Cr.	General, Administrative, and Store Operating Exp.		176,993
Cr.	Provision for Income Taxes		68,040
Cr.	Retained Earnings		102,062

g. Balance Sheet

ABERCROMBIE & FITCH CO.
CONSOLIDATED BALANCE SHEETS
(Thousands)

	January 30, 1999
ASSETS	
CURRENT ASSETS:	
Cash and Equivalents	$163,564
Accounts Receivable	4,101
Inventories	43,992
Store Supplies	5,887
Receivable from The Limited	–
Other	691
TOTAL CURRENT ASSETS	218,235
PROPERTY AND EQUIPMENT, NET	89,558
DEFERRED INCOME TAXES	10,737
OTHER ASSETS	631
TOTAL ASSETS	$319,161
LIABILITIES AND SHAREHOLDERS' EQUITY	
CURRENT LIABILITIES:	
Accounts Payable	$24,759
Accrued Expenses	63,882
Income Taxes Payable	33,587
TOTAL CURRENT LIABILITIES	122,228
LONG-TERM DEBT	–
OTHER LONG-TERM LIABILITIES	10,828
SHAREHOLDERS' EQUITY:	
Common Stock	517
Paid-In Capital	144,142
Retained Earnings	43,131
	187,790
Less: Treasury Stock, at Average Cost	(1,685)
TOTAL SHAREHOLDERS' EQUITY	186,105
TOTAL LIABILITIES AND SHAREHOLDERS' EQUITY	$319,161

h. Sales in fiscal 1998 are up 56% over 1997 (521,617 / 335,372 = 1.56) and up another 56% in fiscal 1999 (815,804 / 521,617 = 1.56). The company is experiencing sales growth which, all else equal, is positive news.

i. In dollar terms, there does not appear to be a pattern with respect to inventory. Inventory was $34,943 in 1997 and dropped 3% to $33,927 in 1998 (33,927 / 34,943 = 0.97). Then, in 1999 inventory climbed 30% to $43,992 (43,992 / 33,927 = 1.30).

But when inventory is scaled (or compared) to total assets a pattern emerges. Relative inventory levels have decreased from 33% in 1997 to 19% in 1998 to 14% for 1999. This indicates a trend toward lower or stable inventory levels, even though sales are increasing significantly. This indicates that the company is becoming more efficient at managing its inventory. In addition, inventory is being sold more quickly —an especially important trend in the fashion industry where tastes can change overnight. In particular, inventory turnover (cost of sales / inventory) has increased over the three years. In terms of average inventory holding period (365 days / inventory turnover) we see a positive trend with holding period dropping from 60 days to 34 days. This reflects increased asset efficiency. The increase in gross margin percent ([sales - cost of sales] / sales) from 36.9% in 1997 to 38.5% in 1998 to 42.2% in 1999 is a further reflection of this increased efficiency.

	1999	1998	1997
Inventory	43,992	33,927	34,943
Cost of Goods Sold, Occupancy & Buying Costs	471,853	320,537	211,606
Total Assets	319,161	183,238	105,761
Inventory as a % of total assets	13.8%	18.5%	33.0%
Inventory Turnover (COGS / Inventory)	10.7 times	9.4 times	6.1 times
Inventory Holding Period (365/ Turnover)	34.0 days	38.6 days	60.3 days

j. Investors would benefit with information about the following:

- An overview of the state of the apparel industry in general. A detailed understanding of how Abercrombie & Fitch's competitors are doing. An assessment of how A&F is doing in context of the overall industry.
- How much of Abercrombie & Fitch's sales increases are attributable to new store openings and how much is attributable to increases in sales from existing stores? "Same store sales" or sales from stores open for at least a year is an important indicator of profitability and growth in the retail industry.
- Can increases due to new store openings be sustained in the long-run?
- The proportion of A&F's manufacturing that occurs off-shore. Domestic labor is more expensive, how is the company affected by cheap imports?
- The company's commitment to design and fashion innovations. What is A&F doing to prevent fashion lines from becoming "stale?"

Teaching Notes:

The capitalize versus expense decision is a fundamental one in accounting. In this case, students consider the appropriateness of a high profile company's capitalization policy. AOL's aggressive capitalization of marketing and software costs was in the news for several years before the company decided to change its policies.

As noted in the accompanying news article, the effect of the change in accounting policy was to wipe out earnings for the past five years!

In addition, the company made a change in accounting estimate during fiscal 1996, extending the amortization period for a class of capitalized costs. In the case, students are asked to estimate the effect of the change on reported earnings. Because the company has also reported the effect, students are able to see that their estimate (based on reasonable assumptions) is quite close to the actual one.

This is a challenging case. We have made a number of assumptions in the questions. Bright students will question the appropriateness of the assumptions. This can be used to start a discussion of the subjectivity of financial analysis.

a. According to AOL, the company capitalizes costs incurred for the production of computer software used in the sale of its services. Costs capitalized include direct labor and related overhead for software produced by the company and the costs of software purchased from third parties. All costs in the software development process which are classified as research and development are expensed as incurred until technological feasibility has been established. Once technological feasibility has been established, such costs are capitalized until the software is commercially available. To the extent the company retains the rights to software development funded by third parties, such costs are capitalized in accordance with the company's normal accounting policies. Amortization is provided on a product-by-product basis, using the greater of the straight-line method or current year revenue as a percent of total revenue estimates for the related software product, not to exceed five years, commencing the month after the date of product release.

b. According to AOL, the company expenses the costs of advertising as incurred, except direct response advertising, which is classified as deferred subscriber acquisition costs. Direct response advertising consists solely of the costs of marketing programs which result in subscriber registrations without further effort required by the company. These costs, which relate directly to subscriber solicitations, principally include the printing, production and shipping of starter kits and the costs of obtaining qualified prospects by various targeted direct marketing programs and from third parties. To date all deferred subscriber acquisition costs have been incurred for the solicitation of specifically identifiable prospects. No indirect costs are included in deferred subscriber acquisition costs.

The deferred costs are amortized, beginning the month after such costs are incurred, over a period determined by calculating the ratio of current revenues related to direct response advertising versus the total expected revenues related to this advertising, or twenty-four months, whichever is shorter. All other costs related to the acquisition of subscribers, as well as general marketing costs, are expensed as incurred.

c. In both cases, one can make the argument that the costs are incurred to generate future benefits and that to better match revenues and expenses, AOL should capitalize the costs and amortize them on a basis that ties the costs to the revenues they generate.

d. The argument against capitalizing these costs is that the link between the costs incurred and the expected revenues is weak. In the face of this high level of uncertainty about the realization of future revenues, many accountants would appeal to the principle of conservatism and expense the costs as they were incurred.

e. It is not correct to argue that conservative accounting is always "good" accounting. For one thing, it leads to poor matching of revenues and expenses. In one period, a company reports expenses and looks less profitable. In a future period, if the revenues actually materialize, then the company looks relatively more profitable.

Some companies are alleged to smooth earnings, or manage earnings, by writing off costs in particularly good years and then not having costs to write off in poor years. This sort of behavior is engaged in to make the managers look like they are in control of the company. That is, the income statements show less volatility in earnings over time than they would if earnings were not smoothed. If smooth earnings are interpreted as less volatile earnings (or management is perceived to be better at controlling the volatility) the company may be able to lower its cost of capital.

f. Data for these accounts comes from note 2.

Product development costs, net

end. bal. 1994	7,912		
capitalized	13,054	2,017	amortized
end. bal. 1995	18,949		
capitalized	32,631	7,250	amortized
end. bal. 1996	44,330		

Product development costs, gross

end. bal. 1994	13,797		
capitalized	13,054		
end. bal. 1995	26,851		
capitalized	32,631		
end. bal. 1996	59,482		

Accumulated Amortization

		5,885	end. bal. 1994
		2,017	amortized
		7,902	end. bal. 1995
		7,250	amortized
		15,152	end. bal. 1996

1996 Entries:

Dr.	Product development costs	32,631	
Cr.	Cash, A/P		32,631

To record product development costs incurred

Dr.	Product development expense	7,250	
Cr.	Accumulated amortization		7,250

To amortize product development costs

g.

Deferred subscriber acquisition costs, net

end. bal. 1994	26,392		
capitalized (SCF)	111,761	60,924	amortized (SCF)
end. bal. 1995	77,229		
capitalized (SCF)	363,024	126,072	amortized (SCF)
end. bal. 1996	314,181		

Dr.	Deferred subscriber acquisition costs	363,024	
Cr.	Cash		363,024

To record subscriber acquisition costs incurred

Dr.	Cost of revenues	126,072	
Cr.	Accumulated amortization		126,072

To amortize subscriber acquisition costs

h. i. AOL did not write off any product development costs as obsolete in 1996.

h. ii.   Amortization as a function of opening balance in gross cost:
1995: 2,017 / 13,797 = 14.6%
1996: 7,250 / 26,851 = 27.0%

Amortization as a function of opening balance in gross cost & additions (smoothed):
1995: 2,017 / (13,797 + 13,054/2) = 9.9%
1996: 7,250 / (26,851 + 32,631/2) = 16.8%

This trend is indicates AOL is amortizing costs more quickly which implies more conservative accounting relating to these costs.

i. i. Per Note 2, the effect was to increase net income by $48,106,000. Thus restated, the net loss would have been $18,290,000 (29,816 - 48,106).

i. ii.   Pretax income (average tax rate): 48,106 / (1 - .52) = 100,221
Pretax income (statutory tax rate): 48,106 / (1 - .35) = 74,009

i. iii.   The quality of AOL's earnings has decreased in light of the change. The costs are now deferred and spread out over a longer period. In a period of intensified competition among Internet providers and high turnover in subscribers, it is not clear whether revenues related to direct response advertising can be adequately assessed to justify capitalization of the costs, never mind extending the amortization period.

i. iv.   If costs incurred in the past had been incurred midway through the respective fiscal year, then costs incurred in fiscal 1994 would have been completely amortized (under the 15 month assumption) by the end of fiscal 1995 and so would not affect amortization in fiscal 1996.

Costs incurred in fiscal 1995 would have been amortized for 6 months, leaving 9 months to amortize. Thus, under the prior amortization period, those costs (representing the *opening* fiscal 1996 balance in the deferred subscriber acquisition costs) would have been amortized in fiscal 1996. The amount is $77,229

Costs incurred in fiscal 1996 would have been amortized for 6 of 15 months under the assumptions in the case. The amount is $363,024 * 6 / 15 = $145,210.

Thus, total amortization under the old assumptions is $222,439.

Under the new 24 month amortization period, the opening balance ($77,229) is going to be amortized over 18 more months (24-6). Therefore, 12 / 18 * $77,229 will be amortized in 1996 ($51,486)

Only 6 / 24 of 1996 capitalized costs of $363,024 will be amortized in 1996 ($90,756)

Thus, the total amortization under the new assumptions is $142,242

Thus, our estimate of the effect of the change in amortization period is $80,197 on a pretax basis, which lies between the two estimates we generated in part i. ii.

j. i.

Reported pretax income	62,339
Write off subscriber acq. costs as incurred	(363,024)
Add back amortization of prior costs	126,072
	(174,613)
Tax benefit @ 52% average tax rate	90,798
Restated Net Income	$(83,815)

j. ii.   Correlating stock price changes and announcements in the financial press is always tricky. Although, AOL announced a big drop in what it would report in earnings, we have shown above that it is possible to make such adjustments on our own. In the past, AOL's accounting had been in the news as aggressive. If analysts had already made the adjustment themselves, then the company's announcement did not really have "information content."

On the other hand, if the market inferred that AOL was no longer going to try to "fool" them with accounting gimmicks, then they might also infer that the reason why is that the future looks bright for AOL and the company no longer needs aggressive accounting to look profitable.

Finally, the stock may have risen due to other factors announced at the same time. AOL announced concurrently several operating and marketing changes. These could be what is responsible for the stock price increase.

Tricky stuff!

AMR Corporation—Leases

Teaching notes:

The distinction between capital and operating leases is subtle. AMR Corporation's (parent company of American Airlines) treatment of its flight equipment provides an excellent example of the technicalities of accounting for leases. The company has both types of leases for the same types of equipment.

This case requires students to ask "What if...?" and to consider how accounting choices affect the quality of a firm's earnings and balance sheets. Firms consider the income statement and balance sheet effects of treating leases as capital vs. operating when they structure lease contracts. Thus, being able to recast the financials to reflect the alternative choice is a useful skill. Specifically, students are required to consider how AMR Corporation's financials would look if all the leases treated as operating had instead been capitalized. The case includes a comparison of various ratios under the two accounting treatments.

Students without a good understanding of present value and the implicit interest rate method will be challenged by this section of the case. A quick refresher is probably in order.

a. Leasing may be more advantageous than purchasing when:

- the lessor needs the asset for only a short time relative to the life of the asset
- the lessor is in a better position to sell the asset when it is no longer needed
- the lessee wants to avoid risks associated with technological obsolescence (i.e. the risk of resale prices being unexpectedly low)
- the lessee wants to avoid risks associated with potential environmental remediation
- the lessee does not want to report additional assets or liabilities on its balance sheet (i.e., to be able to report higher ROA or to avoid breaking restrictive debt covenants)
- it is to the lessee's advantage to deduct rent payments instead of interest and depreciation for tax purposes

Of course, the specific details of a given lease agreement can enhance or eliminate any of these advantages.

b. An **operating lease** is one that does not transfer the risks and benefits of ownership to the lessee. Typically such leases will be short-term (relative to the life of the leased asset). They are what we commonly refer to as rental agreements. For example, if you lease an apartment for one year, it would be hard to argue that you have assumed the risks and benefits of ownership. You don't need to insure the building or pay to fix the roof nor are you able to sell it and receive the proceeds.

Capital leases, on the other hand, are ones where the risk and benefit of ownership are deemed to have been transferred to the lessee. From an accounting perspective, long-term leases (e.g., more than 75% of the estimated useful life of the asset), leases where ownership passes to the lessee at the end of the lease or where there is a "bargain purchase option," or leases where the present value of the lease payments is close to the fair value of the asset (e.g., 90%) are considered capital leases (any one of the four criteria is enough). In essence, if a lease is a capital lease, the lessee effectively owns the asset and is financing it through the lessor. That the lessor maintains the title to the asset is considered an issue of form but not substance.

Capital leases come in several forms. From the point of view of the *lessor*, under a capital lease, there will be no leased asset on its balance sheet. An important issue is whether to recognize a gain or loss on the "sale" of the asset to the lessee. Although the rules are more technical than we allude to here, a **direct financing** lease is one where the present value of the lease payments is equal to the cost of the asset. As such, at the inception of the lease there is no gain or loss recorded by the lessor. With the passage of time, the lessor earns interest revenue (i.e., lease payments are partly interest and partly principal).

Under a **sales-type** lease, the present value of the lease payments is greater than the cost of the asset to the lessor. This may occur when the lessor is a manufacturer (the difference is akin to gross profit) or when the lessor is an intermediary that buys assets in bulk and leases them in smaller quantities (charging the lessee the implicit cost of a smaller quantity purchase). In a sales type lease, at the inception of the lease, the lessor records profit equal to the difference between the book value of the asset and the present value of the lease payments. With the passage of time under the lease, the lessor earns interest revenue.

c. Accountants distinguish between different types of leases because although they are similar in *form* (i.e., a contract to make specified payments and title has not passed to the lessee), in *substance*, an operating lease is not the same as a capital lease. As noted in part b, an operating lease does not transfer the risks and benefits of ownership to the lessee. A capital lease does and, as such, for the financial statements to represent the underlying economics of the contract, an asset and a liability should be shown on the lessee's books.

d.

Dr.   Aircraft rentals   1,012
Cr.   Cash   1,012
To record payments on operating leases for 1999.

e. The flight equipment totaling $13,688 refers to the 482 owned aircraft (375 for American plus 107 for AMR Eagle-see the 10-K excerpt). The other amount, $3,159, is flight equipment under capital leases (86 aircraft for American and 63 aircraft for AMR Eagle). Generally accepted accounting principles require that equipment under capital leases be recorded as a fixed asset and depreciated over its useful life.

f. Using the assumptions of a 5% salvage value and 20 years useful life, depreciation on the owned aircraft is ($13,688 * .95) / 20 = $650.

Dr.   Depreciation and amortization expense   650
Cr.   Accumulated depreciation - flight equipment   650
To record depreciation on owned aircraft for 1998.

For leased aircraft, amortization is $3,159 / 20 = $160.

Dr.   Depreciation and amortization expense   160
Cr.   Accumulated amortization - leased flight equipment   160
To record amortization on capital leased aircraft for 1998 (assumes 20 year lease)

g. The total capital lease obligation amounting to $1,918 (from Note 4) has been classified for presentation purposes. The current portion (that portion due within the next year) is $154 and is shown in the current liability section. The balance of the obligation, $1,764, is the long-term portion and is shown separately.

h. i. The average rate is 6.7695%. This rate can be determined in a variety of ways. The easiest way is to use a calculator or spreadsheet program and calculate the Internal Rate of Return (or IRR) of the cash flows. IRR is simply the rate of return (or interest rate) that makes the present value of a series of cash flows equal zero. In this case, let the present value of the lease payments equal the cash flow at Time 0, and let each of the lease payments equal a negative cash flow at Time 1 through 10.

Alternately, one could calculate the present value of the lease payments and compare that to the present value of the minimum lease payments referred to in Note 4. Using a spreadsheet makes this fairly simple. If we start off using 10% we find that the rate was too high. Using 7% is still high and 6% turns out to be too low. With a little trial and error, we arrive at 6.7695%. The table below illustrates the effect of using different rates to discount the lease payments.

Interest Rate	Present Value
10%	1,672
7%	1,899
6%	1,985
6.5%	1,941
6.7695%	1,918

h. ii. The effective interest rate method uses the 6.7695% we calculated above. We can use this rate to set up a lease amortization table. Each lease payment covers interest and principal on the lease obligation. The following amortization table shows how each payment is split between principal and interest. The question did not require you to calculate this table. It is provided here for completeness. In 1999, we see from column 2 that interest will be $130.

Year	column 1 Payment	Column 2 Interest Expense (beg bal. * .0677)	column 3 Reduction in Obligation (col.1 - col.2)	column 4 Remaining Lease Balance (beg bal. - col.3)
1998	Beginning bal.			1918
1999	273	130	143	1775
2000	341	120	221	1554
2001	323	105	218	1336
2002	274	90	184	1152
2003	191	78	113	1039
2004	252	70	182	857
2005	252	58	194	663
2006	252	45	207	456
2007	252	31	221	235
2008	252	17	235	0

h. iii.   During 1999, cash payments will be $273.

h. iv.
Dr.   Interest Expense (1,918 * .067695)   130
Dr.   Lease Liability ($273-130)   143
Cr.   Cash (annual payment)   273
To record 1999 annual payment made on the capitalized flight equipment leases.

h. v. The 1999 "reduction in obligation" in column 3 is $143 which does not tie into the "current portion of capital lease" on the balance sheet, $154. It should. It doesn't because of the way we calculated the effective interest rate in the previous part of the question. For simplicity, we assumed that all the payments were made at the end of the respective years. AMR Corporation probably has to make payments throughout the year. If that is the case then the "true" effective rate is somewhat higher than the 6.7695% that we came up with. Using a slightly higher rate means that a greater portion of the $273 million payment in 1999 relates to interest and therefore a smaller portion relates to the annual lease principal reduction—making the difference between our estimate and the reported number larger. However, we also assumed that the payments subsequent to 2003 were evenly spread over 5 years. Had we used a longer time period, the interest rate would have dropped and the principal payment would have been larger in 1999. Finally, we calculated an average over all the leases. The rate that AMR Corporation actually uses to capitalize each lease at its inception may not be constant over all the leases.

i. i. The present value of the future cash payments must be calculated to determine the amount that would have been capitalized. At 8% this amount is $7,816.

i. ii.
Dr.   Flight Equipment at cost   7,816
Cr.   Obligation under capital lease   7,816
To capitalize flight equipment leases.

i. iii.
Flight Equipment, at cost
    Before capitalization   3,159
    Newly capitalized operating leases   <u>7,816</u>
    Pro Forma Balance Sheet number   <u>10,975</u>

```
Total Assets
    Before capitalization                                22,303
    Newly capitalized operating leases                    7,816
    Pro Forma Balance Sheet number                       30,119
```

i. iv.

```
Total Liabilities
    Before capitalization                                15,605
    Newly capitalized operating leases                    7,816
    Pro Forma Balance Sheet number                       23,421

Total Current Liabilities
    Before capitalization                                 5,639
    Current portion of newly capitalized
        operating leases ($1,012 - ($7,816 * 8%))           387
    Pro Forma Balance Sheet number                        6,026

Obligations under capital lease - long-term portion
    Before capitalization                                 1,764
    Non-current portion of newly capitalized
        operating leases ($7,816 - $387)                  7,429
    Pro Forma Balance Sheet number                        9,193
```

i. v. One reason AMR's management would like to report aircraft leases as operating leases is that doing so keeps both assets and liabilities off the balance sheet. As a result, for a given level of net income, profitability measures such as ROA will be higher. In addition, the Debt-Equity ratio will be lower. Both of these will lead more favorable interpretations of the company—unless, of course, financial statement users adjust for the effects!

Another reason for structuring the leases as operating leases is so that the company has increased financial flexibility. For example, consider the covenants referred to in Note 3 to the financial statements which indicate that the company would face interest rates between one half percent and seven percent higher than the stated rates on the leases if the credit rating on certain debentures should fall. To the extent that keeping debt "off the balance sheet" helps avoid such downgrades, operating leases would be preferred to capital ones.

j.

	1998 As Reported	Pro Forma (Capitalize @ year-end)
Income after tax	1,314	1,314
Current assets	4,875	4,875
Total assets	22,303	30,119
Current liabilities	5,639	6,026
Total liabilities	15,605	23,421
Total equity	6,698	6,698
Interest expense	372	372
Income tax rate	39.5%	39.5%
Current ratio	4,875/5,639 = 0.86	4,875/6,026 = 0.51
Return on Assets (ROA)	(1,314+372(1-.395))/22,303 = 0.069	(1,314+372(1-.395))/30,119 = 0.051
Return on Equity (ROE)	1,314/6,698 = 0.196	1,314/6,698 = 0.196
Debt to equity ratio	15,605/6,698 = 2.33	23,421/6,698 = 3.50

ROA = net income + interest expense (1 - tax rate) / total assets
ROE = net income / stockholders' equity
current ratio = current assets / current liabilities
debt to equity = total liabilities / total stockholders' equity

Had AMR's flight equipment under operating leases been capitalized, risk, solvency, and profitability ratios would all worsen. This deterioration of ratios is why many companies strive to obtain "off-balance sheet financing."

This type of financing (i.e., operating lease accounting) keeps both the asset and (more importantly) the liability off the balance sheet.

Although adding debt to the balance sheet always hurts the liquidity, solvency/risk ratios, the effect on the income statement of capitalizing leases in more complex. The total cash flow of a lease (whether operating or capital) is the same, but the pattern of expenses will differ across the years. That is, the total rent expense (operating lease) will equal the total interest and amortization expense (capital lease). However, in the early years of a capital lease a greater portion of the lease payment will cover interest expense and the sum of interest expense and depreciation will likely exceed the year's cash flow (or rental expense). This will be especially true if accelerated depreciation is used. In later years the difference will reverse.

Analog Devices, Inc.—Revenue Recognition

Teaching Notes:

The focus of this case is revenue recognition. We begin by looking at general definitions of revenues and gains, followed by definitions of revenue recognition. Students are asked to assess when revenue should be recognized for a service provider (movie theater), a retailer (record store), a manufacturer (publisher), and finally for ADI—a designer and manufacturer of analog, mixed signal, and digital signal processing integrated circuits.

In 1998, ADI changed its revenue recognition policy for international sales. Proforma information in the notes to the financial statements allows students to see the effect of the change on current and prior period financial statements. As not all the required data are provided, reasonable estimates need to be made to determine the effect of the change on gross margins.

By analyzing the reported and proforma trends in revenues and earnings, students gain the ability to assess the relation between accounting choices and earnings quality.

a. According to the FASB's conceptual framework (Statement of Concepts No. 6: Elements of Financial Statements), revenues are "… inflows or other enhancements of assets of an entity or settlements of its liabilities (or a combination of both) from delivering or producing goods, rendering services, or other activities that constitute the entity's ongoing major or central operations."

"Gains are increases in equity (net assets) from peripheral or incidental transactions of an entity and from all other events or circumstances affecting the entity except those that result from revenues or investments by owners."

The statement goes on to say, "Revenue and gains are similar, and expenses and losses are similar, but some differences are significant in conveying information about an enterprise's performance. Revenues and expenses result from an entity's ongoing major or central operations and activities—that is, from activities such as producing or delivering goods, rendering services, lending, insuring, investing, and financing. In contrast, gains and losses result from incidental or peripheral transactions of an enterprise with other entities and from other events and circumstances affecting it. Some gains and losses may be considered "operating" gains and losses and may be closely related to revenues and expenses. Revenues and expenses are commonly displayed as gross inflows or outflows of net assets, while gains and losses are usually displayed as net inflows or outflows."

b. When a company "recognizes" revenues it records a journal entry involving a debit to cash or receivables (sometimes to deferred revenues) and a credit to a revenue account. That is, it 'books a sale.'

According to the FASB's conceptual framework (Statement of Concepts No. 5: Recognition and Measurement in Financial Statements of Business Enterprises), revenues are "… generally not recognized until realized or realizable. Revenues … are realized when products (goods or services), merchandise, or other assets are exchanged for cash or claims to cash. Revenues … are realizable when related assets received or held are readily convertible to known amounts of cash or future claims to cash. Revenues are not recognized until earned. An entity's revenue-earning activities involve delivering or producing goods, rendering services, or other activities that constitute its ongoing major or central operations, and revenues are considered to have been earned when the entity has substantially accomplished what it must do to be entitled to the benefits represented by the revenues. …"

In plain English, the criteria for revenue recognition are (1) the company has done the work, (2) they know how much the work cost, (3) they know how much they are going to get paid, and (4) they are reasonably sure of getting it.

c. A movie theater usually renders its service to customers within a couple hours of selling tickets. Therefore, movie theaters recognize most of their revenues concurrently with the receipt of cash. Some theaters sell gift certificates that represent future revenues. These items should be recorded as a liability representing the obligation to provide a service in the future. When the coupons are used, the liability turns into revenue.

d. A recorded-music store usually would recognize revenues at the sales counter, when payment is received for merchandise. In recent years, many of stores have instituted liberal sales-return policies. These policies increase the uncertainty of whether a sale has actually occurred. When the right of return exists, a business must estimate the amount of future returns and deduct that amount from the current period revenues.

e. A publisher likely will recognize sales revenue when the books are shipped. Because the customer usually pays for shipping, they are said to be in "constructive receipt" of the merchandise while it is in transit.

f. If a bookstore can return unsold books, the publisher should make an estimate of future returns and deduct it from the current period's sales. If a customer is unable to pay for merchandise that is shipped, it has no affect on the recognized revenues. However, an estimate for uncollectible accounts is deducted from accounts receivable and is recognized as an expense in the income statement. This estimate of bad debts should be "matched" with the revenue that resulted in the uncollectible account.

g. Revenue should be recognized when the earnings process is substantially complete. Normally, that means that the seller has done the work, knows what the selling price is, is reasonably sure of getting paid the selling price (adjusted for discounts and returns), and knows what the product or service cost. For ADI, the sales process is complete when they have shipped goods to their customers. If there is substantial uncertainty about the likelihood of having goods returned to the company (i.e., they don't really know how much they will eventually collect), then ADI should defer the recognition of revenue until that uncertainty is reduced. When ADI can reasonably estimate the expected sales returns, they can record the net sales.

h.

Dr.	Accounts receivable	1,450,379
Cr.	Net sales	1,450,379

To record revenues for the year.

i. In 1998, ADI changed its revenue recognition policy to a more conservative one. In the past, they had a mixed policy where they recognized revenue immediately when product was shipped to their international distributors. Because those shipments could be returned to ADI (perhaps due to lack of demand or technological obsolescence of the chips), ADI recorded a concurrent reserve for product returns and discounts on those sales. For most domestic sales, ADI deferred revenue when their products were shipped to distributors and waited until the chips were resold to end users. This eliminated the uncertainty surrounding the estimation of a reserve for returns and discounts.

In 1998, they adopted the more-conservative deferral of revenue policy for both domestic and international sales on the grounds that it better conforms to the substance of the transaction considering the changing business environment in the international marketplace (we are led to assume that, internationally, a more liberal return and discount policy environment may have arisen), the policy is consistent with industry practice, and it better focuses the sales force on serving end-users.

It is interesting to note that this more-conservative practice actually helps improve the appearance of ADI's sales trend. If analysts focus on the proforma sales figures, the company reports an increase in sales from 1997 to 1998.

j. i. Comparing ADI's reported revenues and profits for the period 1997 to 1999 is challenging because of the change in revenue recognition policy. The 1997 figures report revenues and earnings on the old basis, the 1998 figures report revenues on the new basis but include a cumulative adjustment to prior periods' earnings (net of tax) for the accounting change in the current period earnings, and the 1999 revenue and earnings figures are based on the new policy.

A diligent reader needs to use the proforma figures from Note 5 to generate comparable data for the period. Unfortunately, ADI only provides high-level figures. They do not restate the entire income statement, nor do they provide balance sheet effects.

j. ii.   The following table summarizes the reported and proforma revenues and earnings for the period 1997 to 1999.

	1997	1998	1999
Net sales, as reported	1,243,494	1,230,571	1,450,379
Proforma net sales	1,214,602	1,230,571	1,450,379
Net income, as reported	178,219	82,408	196,819
Proforma net income	167,515	119,488	196,819
Growth in reported net sales		-1.0%	17.9%
Growth in proforma net sales		1.3%	17.9%
Growth in reported NI		-53.8%	138.8%
Growth in proforma NI		-28.7%	64.7%

The growth rate in revenues from 1997 to 1998 is pretty weak no matter how it is evaluated. The semiconductor industry was in a slump that year and ADI was certainly not immune. Revenues grew a meager 1.3% on a proforma basis which is better than the reported decrease of 1.0%. In 1999, revenues rose 17.9% (there is no difference between reported and proforma as the proforma figures for revenues only affect 1997).

The differences in the trends in earnings are more significant. Reported NI, as the semiconductor industry came out of its slump, grew 139%. The growth is enhanced due to the one-time cumulative effect of accounting change that reduced 1998 NI. On a proforma basis, the company's NI grew a healthy 65%.

One might question whether the decision to change accounting policies was made opportunistically. That is, 1998 was a poor year by any measure. By changing the revenue recognition policy to a more conservative one in that year, ADI afforded itself the opportunity to shift revenues into *future* periods. When the semiconductor industry pulled out of its downturn, the company was poised to report huge growth in both revenues and profits. A key question that needs answering is whether the reported growth in revenues is due to selling more product in 1999 or due to the shifting of revenues from prior periods into 1999. An astute analyst will ask management for a breakdown or perform an analysis of the deferred revenue accounts. A deep understanding of the economics underlying the reported revenues will help generate better evaluations of past performance and more accurate forecasts of future performance.

j. iii.   To determine the effect of the accounting change on gross margins, we need to determine what 1997 net sales and cost of goods sold would have been under the new accounting policy. ADI provides us with the proforma net sales and net income figures but not the cost of goods sold data. However, by making some reasonable assumptions, we can work backwards to a reasonable estimate of COGS.

The following analysis assumes that the tax rate reported in the 1997 income statement holds for the proforma financials. In addition, it is reasonable to assume that the operating expenses (and equity in WaferTech loss and nonoperating expenses) are unchanged by the accounting change.

Proforma net income	$167,515
Estimated taxes at 24.4%	(40,874)
Estimated income before tax	221,581
Less nonoperating income	(2,463)
Less WaferTech equity income	(214)
Add Operating expenses	387,761
Estimated Gross Margin	606,665
Proforma Net Sales	1,214,602
Cost of sales	607,937

1997 Gross margin as reported: 49.93%
1997 Gross margin as a percent of proforma sales: 606,665 / 1,214,602 = 49.94%
1998 Gross margin: 47.8%
1999 Gross margin: 49.3%

Overall the accounting change had no effect on 1997 gross margin as a percentage of sales. The trend in gross margin is up and down. It dropped significantly in 1998 as production fell and increased in 1999 as sales rose and cost controls reduced production costs (per MD&A).

j. iv.   The accounting change affects the 1997 and 1998 balance sheets as follows. The cumulative effect of change in accounting principle reported on the 1998 income statement shows the after-tax effect of the accounting change. Had ADI used the new policy in 1997, they would have reported lower sales and cost of goods sold (and less income tax expense). This would affect the balance sheet via a reduction in retained earnings, a reduction in deferred income taxes (assuming no change in tax payable), an increase in deferred revenues and an increase in inventories.

Assuming the gross margin we derived in part iii. and the taxes associated with the change in policy reported on the 1998 income statement, we can estimate the following changes to the 1997 balance sheet:

Retained earnings lower by $37,080
Deferred taxes lower by $20,000
Deferred revenues higher by $114,297 (57,080 / .4994)
Inventories higher by $57,217

The 1998 balance sheet already uses the new policy and thus, requires no adjustments.

Teaching Notes:

Bally has a wide assortment of debentures and notes that provide a nice way to discuss many of the more common long-term debt features. At the introductory level, bond accounting is kept straightforward.

Students ought to know how to calculate present value and periodic interest payments. Some students will need a present value refresher. The journal entry to accrue interest may trip some students up. Drawing a time-line helps.

Interestingly, Bally's recent stock price drops are in evidence in their debt footnote. The 8% debentures issued during the year had a conversion price of $12.26, less than half of the price on the 6% debentures for which they were exchanged. Although the case does not include this detail, the fact can be introduced to start a discussion of how debt and equity are priced by the market.

a. i.   Convertible means that the notes can be exchanged or converted to common stock of Bally at the discretion of the holder.

The notes are subordinated which implies they are less senior than other debt issued by Bally. In the event that Bally were to declare bankruptcy, holders of these notes would be paid after higher ranking claims were settled.

Debentures are uncollateralized notes. That is, they are unsecured. In the event of default, debenture holders stand in line behind all the creditors who have specific assets tied to their loans and behind all creditors who have contracted to be paid back ahead of the unsecured creditors.

a. ii.   Sinking funds are monies set aside to pay back financial obligations. Generally, funds are set aside with trustee who invests the money so that the bonds can be paid off or repurchased. Some bond contracts require sinking funds in order to reduce the risk of default.

b. i.   Adding the unamortized discount ($1,678) to the net number ($273,322) reveals that the face value of these debentures is $275,000.

b. ii.   Interest paid to the note holders is calculated using the face value of the notes and the stated rate of interest. $275,000 * .10625 = $29,218.75.

b. iii.

Dr. Interest expense	29,365	
Cr. Cash		29,219
Cr. Unamortized discount		146

To record interest expense for the year.

b. iv.   Interest expense is calculated using the effective interest rate method. That is, interest expense is the net book value of the debentures times the effective rate. From the journal entry above, we know the interest expense and the net book value of the debentures is given in the footnote. Therefore, the effective interest rate is $29,365/273,176 = 10.75%.

c. i.

Dr. Long term borrowing	5,000	
Cr. Cash		4,697
Cr. Other revenues		303

To record the retirement of debentures to satisfy sinking fund requirement.

Details of this transaction are provided in the narrative portion of the note.

c. ii.   The price of the debentures had dropped presumably because the stated (or coupon) interest rate of 10% was lower than what the market demanded for debentures of like risk. This drove the price of the debentures below face value; they were purchased by Bally at a discount.

d. i.

Dr. Long-term debt - 6% Convertible debentures	13,586	
Cr. Long-term debt - 8% Convertible debentures		13,586

To record issuance of 8% debentures in exchange for 6% debentures.

d. ii.   The footnote discloses that shares of stock would be issued in exchange for the 6% debentures at a price of $26.10. The outstanding debentures could be converted to 69,118.8 shares. Rounding down, and assuming that cash is disbursed for the balance, Bally would have prepared the following journal entry.

```
Dr.    6% Convertible Debentures                                    1,804
Cr.         Common Stock, Par (69,118 shares at 66.67 cents)              46.08
Cr.         Capital in Excess of Par                                   1,757.90
Cr.         Cash                                                             .02
```
To record conversion of 6% debentures to common stock.

e. i.   The net book value of these notes did not change year-over-year. This implies that there is no discount or premium on them. Hence, they were issued at par. Because they pay interest semi-annually, the effective annual rate on the notes is:

$$\left(1+\frac{9.25\%}{2}\right)^2 - 1 = 9.464\%$$

e. ii.   Because interest is not paid until a month after year end, five month's worth of interest must be accrued at year end. In January when the interest is paid, the accrual is reversed for the five months and one month's interest (January 1996) is recorded.

December 31, 1995
```
Dr.    Interest expense                                             16,380
Cr.         Accrued interest (current liability)                           16,380
```
*To accrue 5 months of interest. ($425,000 * 9.25%/2 * 5/6 = 16,380)*

January 31, 1996
```
Dr.    Interest expense                                              3,276
Dr.    Accrued interest (current liability)                         16,380
Cr.         Cash                                                           19,656
```
*To record semi-annual interest payment. ($425,000 * 9.25%/2 * 6/6 = 19,656)*

BCE Inc.—Investments in Other Companies

Teaching Notes:

This case shows students how the equity method of accounting works. The note disclosures made by BCE in 1990 are rarely seen. In fact, BCE has not included the information in Note 4 in subsequent years. The financials provide a textbook example of how the equity method works.

Students have little trouble determining how BCE accounts for its 20-50% owned subsidiaries. They find it much more challenging to trace the effects thereof through the financial statements. The accompanying solution spells out the obvious and not so obvious relationships in detail.

a. BCE is a holding company. That is, BCE does not engage in the manufacture or sale of telecom equipment or services. Rather, it owns a number of operating companies that do. Some of the companies are 100% owned, others are partially owned. That way, BCE can control (or significantly influence) the subsidiaries and associated companies. By retaining less than 100% ownership, BCE effectively finances the companies it controls with other investors' money.

b. i. Note 1 states that investments in associated companies (20% to 50% owned) are accounted for by the equity method.

b. ii. Using the equity method, the investor company (i) initially records the investment at the cost of acquiring shares in the investee; (ii) records in each subsequent period (usually at year-end), an increase in the investment balance for its share of the investee's earnings (a decrease for its share of any losses); (iii) and records any dividends paid by the investee as a reduction in the investment balance because dividends represent a distribution of the investee's net equity.

(i) Dr. Investment in Company
     Cr. Cash
To record initial acquisition of shares.

(ii) Dr. Investment in Company
      Cr. Income from Associated Company
To record proportionate share of investee earnings accrued.

(iii) Dr. Cash
      Cr. Investment in Company
To record receipt of dividends distributed by investee.

c. In BCE's case, the proportionate share of the net income is included in the Income Statement in "Equity in net income of associated companies" [+155] and in the Balance Sheet account "Investments in Associated Companies" (see I/S and Note 4, respectively).

Dividends paid by the associated companies are included in cash and reduce the "Investments in Associated Companies" [-106]. The Statement of changes in financial position (the cash flow statement) shows that only BCE's equity in the net income of associated companies in excess of dividends received is subtracted from BCE's net income to determine cash received by BCE [155 (part of net income) - 49 (SCF adjustment to NI) = 106 (cash dividends received)]. That is a complicated way of showing that only dividends received from associated companies affected cash!

d.
(i) Dr. Associated Companies (at equity)   155
     Cr. Equity in Net Income of Associated Companies   155
To record proportionate share of investee earnings accrued.

(ii) Dr. Cash   106
      Cr. Associated Companies (at equity)   106
To record receipt of dividends distributed by investee.

e. Because BCE no longer maintained "significant influence" (as defined by GAAP) over the operations of Encor (its ownership level dropped to 19.3%), it switched from using the equity method to using the cost method. Because BCE no longer has "significant influence" in the voting at Encor, its participation in and accounting for income from Encor is limited to the amount of dividends to be received in the future. Note that although we can only speculate, it is not likely a coincidence that BCE owns just slightly less than 20% of Encor. At 19.3% they can use the cost method, and record investment earnings based on Encor's dividends rather than Encor's net income (while still exerting some influence).

f. This is not considered a change in accounting principle. Rather, it reflects a change in economic circumstances and is, therefore, accounted for prospectively as with other changes in circumstances.

Teaching Notes:

Pension accounting is a complicated topic. While the treatment here is at an introductory level, acquiring basic pension terminology is still quite a task. Bethlehem's pension liability shows rather dramatically how pension accounting under SFAS 87 (and the associated SFAS 106) can yield puzzling results. Although the company has an under-funded pension plan of $25 million, the balance sheet shows a liability of $410 million. The difference in the "other benefits" arena is even larger.

The case begins with an introduction to pension vocabulary and assumptions. Once students build up their pension lexicon, they are ready to tackle the balance sheet and income statement effect of pension plan accounting.

It should be clear to students, as they proceed through the case, that accounting for pensions takes the employer's perspective. The pension plan assets are NOT under the company's economic control, they are managed by a separate pension fund. Thus, the company does not record (directly) changes in the fair value of the plan assets, income from the asset transactions, or the cash disbursed to retirees.

Some students may have difficulty understanding why Bethlehem does not record the full difference between its pension obligations and the fair value of its pension assets as a liability. The questions that deal with the other components of the pension liability calculation should clear this up. This remains the most confusing part of pension accounting for most students.

The case can be expanded by introducing a discussion of the potential economic consequences of recording pension assets and liabilities in full on the balance sheet. This could lead to an exploration of the political nature of the standard setting process.

a. The two types of pension plans are defined-contribution and defined-benefit. An employer with a defined-contribution plan pays into the plan either an annual lump-sum per employee or calculates payments based on the employees' current wages and or time of service with the firm. Under such a plan, the employer does not guarantee the future amounts employees will receive when they retire. The employees covered by a defined-contribution plan assume the risk for the pension plan's financial performance.

Under a defined-benefit plan, the employer specifies the size and timing of the payments that the employees will receive when they retire. Typically, these retirement benefits are commensurate with the wages earned by the employee in his or her last few years of employment and a function of the employee's years of service. The employer must fund the plan sufficiently to meet these future obligations. Under a defined-benefit plan, the employer assumes the risk for the plan's performance.

According to the footnote, Bethlehem has a defined-benefit plan.

b. Pension accounting by the employer (e.g., Bethlehem) illustrates the matching principle in that benefit obligations are recorded at their present value when they are earned by the employees. That is, an accrual is made. Cash basis accounting for pensions (which is not permitted) would not record the obligation or the associated expense when the employees worked. Rather, there would be an expense when pension payments were made which might be many years after the employee retired. The expense would not be well matched with the benefits that the employee generated under cash basis accounting for pensions.

c. The obligation increases as a result of pension expense (the service and interest components) as well as actuarial changes in assumptions (i.e., lowering the discount rate or increasing the rate of wage increases) and plan amendments. The obligation decreases when benefits are paid and when actuarial changes reduce the present value of the expected future payments.

d. The pension plan's assets increase when contributions are made to the plan (either by the employer or the employees) and when the assets earn a return (interest, dividends, capital appreciation). Pension benefits are paid out when employees retire and reduce the plan's assets. When securities invested drop in value, the plan's assets fall, too.

e. A number of assumptions are required to estimate the projected pension benefits including the number of expected years of employee service, the rate of wage increase, the mortality rate among employees, the age at retirement, and the discount rate at which the present value of the obligation is calculated.

f. i. The present value of the pension obligation at December 31, 1999 is $6,115 million. This amount is netted against pension plan assets of $6,090 and various unrecognized gains and losses so that the balance sheet recognizes an obligation of $410 million (all in long-term Pension Liability).

f. ii. The projected benefit obligation is underfunded by $25 ($340) at December 31, 1999 (1998). (We ignore the one month difference between the date of the actuarial valuations and the financial statements).

f. iii. The unrecognized net actuarial gain (loss) is the cumulative effect of changing pension plan assumptions about expected service cost, mortality, and returns on plan assets. Recently, this balance has been growing as the pension plan assets are earning more than the long-run expected return. This balance is smoothed into pension expense when it exceeds certain defined amounts. Otherwise, it is untouched and fluctuates from year to year. The idea behind not including the amounts directly into expense is that some of the estimates offset each other over time and introducing yearly changes into earnings would create volatility. If that volatility was managed (i.e., reduced), it might not be in the long-run interest of the pension plan participants. Thus, the rules are designed to smooth the ups and downs.

The initial net obligation is the remainder of the amount by which Bethlehem's pension plan was underfunded when SFAS No. 87 was introduced. That amount is being amortized at $34 per year and will be eliminated in about two years.

The unrecognized service from plan amendments arises when companies change their pension plans (normally sweetening them). The amounts are amortized over the remaining service lives of the employees. This is another smoothing mechanism. If a firm enhances its pension, the workers will be 'happier' and presumably work harder over the remainder of their careers. The cost of the enhancement is matched to those working years.

None of the three amounts shows up on the balance sheet as obligations or assets until they are amortized. As such, although the amounts figure in the calculation of plan obligations and assets, they do not appear in the financial statements themselves.

g. i. At the beginning of the year the plan assets had a value of $5,915. the actual return was $709 or 12%. The expected return was 9.00% for the year. The difference was added to the unrecognized net actuarial gain.

g. ii. In 1998, the "Lukens acquisition" lead to an increase in the projected benefit obligation of $460 with plan assets of only $425 being added. Thus, the Lukens plan was underfunded.

h. i. The key components that make up Bethlehem's Pension expense for the year are:
- Current service cost—the present value of the future benefits earned this year by employees. GE offsets this with contributions made by employees.
- Interest cost—the increase in the cost of the future benefits as they become closer to being paid (i.e., the unraveling of prior discounting of future costs).
- Offsetting the previous two items is the expected return on plan assets—the expected earnings on the amount in the pension plan. Note that this is not the actual amount earned. In any case, the plan assets are expected to earn more than the interest and current service cost combined. In effect, this leads to net pension income (before the following amortizations).
- Amortization of the prior service cost—when a plan is changed the change in the obligation is brought into the expense over time.
- Amortization of the transition gain (initial net obligation)—when SFAS No. 87 was enacted, firms with plan assets less than obligations set up a 'transition loss' (off the firm's books). It is amortized into the expense over the remaining service lives of the employees. When SFAS No. 106 was adopted, the same could happen. Most firms had huge net liabilities but opted to book the cost and liability immediately. Bethlehem was one of those firms and has no transition obligation for its OPEB costs.
- Net actuarial gain recognized—this is where prior differences between expected and actual returns on plan assets and changes in actuarial assumptions and experience rates get smoothed into income. Bethlehem has no changes to amortize.
- Finally, Bethlehem has a variety of other sundry obligations that affect pension expense and are captured under the PBGC, Multiemployer, other heading.

h. ii. The 1999 pension expense was $40 million.

i. By increasing the discount rate on the pension obligation, the ending obligation is decreased. We see in the reconciliation of the obligation that the effect was to reduce it $254 million (including the effect discussed in part *i.*).

j. By reducing the expected salary increases from 3.10% to 2.90% the projected benefit obligation is again decreased.

k.   Bethlehem Steel's pension costs have been decreasing steadily since 1997. This is due in large part to the bull market in U.S. equities which has led to large increases in plan assets. Income from operations has been steadily declining over the same period but would have been even worse had pension expense remained at the 1997 level. (Operating profit would have been 65% lower in 1999 has the 1997 level of pension cost been incurred.) Most analysts do not value reductions in pension costs (and thus improvements in earnings) as highly as improvements due to increases in sales or improved operating efficiencies. If the stock market moves back to more traditional growth levels, Bethlehem may have to begin making significant contributions to the plan assets in order to fund it.

Teaching notes:

This case usually starts a lively class discussion. The economic consequences of FASB pronouncements have been widely debated in the press. OPEB was a very contentious topic and sparked quite a debate. Similarly, the attempt (subsequently defeated) by the FASB to require expensing of stock options awarded to employees as part of compensation packages has been a hot issue.

Students will take both sides of the argument on whether the market will penalize companies for the large hit to earnings in the year of adoption and for the large liability that results.

An important issue to raise (if a student does not) is that corporations manage what they measure. Because corporations did not have to measure OPEB expenses prior to SFAS 106, they were perhaps not properly managing the expense. The enforced measurement and disclosure of the liability may result in employers cutting back on employee benefits. The question is whether not quantifying the number makes the liability go away.

Black Clawson—Other Post–Employment Benefits

a. Under SFAS 106, firms have to accrue post-retirement benefits other than pensions expected to be paid to active and retired employees and their beneficiaries for services rendered by the employees. In general, the treatment is consistent with that of any other obligation of the company, particularly that of deferred compensation (i.e., pensions).

The first year to which the standard applied was 1992. The financial statements of most large corporations showed huge drops in income that year. For many corporations, the OPEB accrual became by far their largest reported liability.

b. The common alternative used by most companies prior to SFAS 106 was the "pay-as-you-go" method, or charging only cash payments to current retirees against income. As you can imagine, this kept a significant liability off the balance sheet. How could this have been allowed? For the most part, companies were not legally obligated to make the payments (even though they almost always did), thus no liability was booked.

c.

Dr.	Other Post Employment Expenses, net of tax*	132,000,000
Dr.	Deferred Tax Assets	68,000,000
Cr.	Liability for Other Post Employment Benefits	200,000,000

To record SFAS No. 106 liability.

*Recorded on the income statement as the cumulative effect of a change in accounting policy.

d. The journal entry does not involve cash. There is no direct cash effect from the accrual of these expenses. The cash outflow associated with this liability is the same as before it was booked; payments are made to employees (or to health care providers) as they incur expenses. The liability is the present value of these estimated future cash outflows.

Although there is no direct cash effect there may be an indirect one. Most corporations were not estimating this huge liability prior to the FASB requiring it. The very act of measuring the liability may have an effect on corporations' willingness to assume new debt or start new projects. That cannot be blamed on the accounting standard (or on the standard setters) rather, it is a management issue.

e. Mr. Landegger seems to take the view that financial statements should ignore economic reality. Perhaps this is too harsh an interpretation, but how else does one characterize his unwillingness to recognize all of the firm's liabilities on the balance sheet? The impact on the firm's credit lines (and any future expansions) should only be affected if the recognized liability was in fact unknown, or underestimated, by those relying on the company's financial statements. Mr. Landegger seems to believe that the users of his financials are not able to back the huge liability out if they want to compare the new financial statements to those of prior years. Unless recognition of the liability impairs the company's ability to finance R & D, such expenditures should not be curtailed as a result of SFAS 106.

A possible economic consequence of the standard to Black Clawson involves debt and compensation contracts. To the extent that such contracts are written in terms of reported Financial Statement ratios and results, debt covenants might be violated (e.g., the debt equity ratio becomes too high) or bonuses might not be earned (e.g., the new expenses lead to income below the lower bound of "required" income levels for bonuses to kick in).

A recent study of the economic consequences of SFAS 106 (Mittelstaedt, Nichols, and Regier: SFAS No. 106 and Benefit Reductions in Employer-Sponsored Retiree Health Care Plans; *The Accounting Review*, October 1995) concluded:

> … Three explanations for … benefit reduction decisions are examined: (1) increased contracting cost caused by the financial reporting consequences of SFAS No. 106, (2) financial weakness independent of SFAS No. 106 and (3) firm-specific increases in retiree health case costs. Strong support for the increased contracting cost hypothesis is found … However, the results also indicate that firms cutting benefits are financially weaker and have higher retiree health care costs at the time the benefits are reduced. Therefore, SFAS No. 106 cannot be viewed as the sole cause of the health care benefit reductions.

Teaching Notes:

In this case, students are asked to perform a financial statement analysis of two companies that compete in the same industry. The case brings to bear all the analytic tools students have acquired over the prior cases.

The questions in this case are meant more as guidelines than as requirements. This should be pointed out to the class in advance. Many students will bring a lot more to the case than asked. Some of them will seek additional sources of information and do industry analyses. Others will compute pro-forma ratios by restating balance sheet and income statement items to be comparable across the two companies. The class can be very instructive if students are encouraged to go beyond the questions asked.

These two companies compete with each other in some markets (in particular, the craft beer segment of the beer market). However, in many ways the companies differ. For example, Boston Beer has adopted a strategy of employing contract brewers to produce its beers. It markets the product nationwide and spends considerable sums on advertising and promotion. Lion produces its own beers as well as several other beverage products. They sell their products regionally in the Northeast U.S. Consequently, the two companies are predicted to have different common-size balance sheets (due to their differing asset bases) and income statements (due to the different margins the various products command and the relative emphasis on advertising).

This case can be used as a springboard to a more general discussion about financial statement analysis. Published annual reports are the primary source of information for financial analysts (Financial Executives Research Foundation, 1987, *Investor Information Needs and the Annual Report*, Morristown, NJ). A class discussion surrounding the purpose of financial statement analysis in investor and creditor judgments and decisions can be started with the following types of questions to students: What are the limitations of financial statement analysis? Should an investor expect to earn abnormally high returns by analyzing financial statement information? Why or why not? What do investors want to know when they evaluate a company? What do creditors want to know? Can these parties find information relevant to these goals in historical-cost based financial statement information?

Note: *the answers to the questions posed in the case are interspersed throughout the discussion that follows.*

Analyzing a company's financial statements involves more than simply calculating a series of ratios and looking at trends. High quality analyses need to be placed in context. That is, an understanding of the company's economic environment and its competitive strategy are essential starting points for interpreting the ratios. In addition, prudent analysts will ask whether the data reflect the underlying economics of the company prior to conducting their analyses. Simply jumping into the data without considering its quality invites two possible deleterious outcomes. First, there may be weaknesses in GAAP that result in a mismatch between the data and economic reality (i.e., GAAP requires that R&D be written off immediately). Second, management may have used the flexibility afforded by GAAP to advance their own self-interest at the expense of other users of the financial statements. As such, we begin our analysis here with an overview of the craft beer industry and the two companies' strategies. We follow that with a look at their accounting policies prior to engaging in the actual financial analysis.

Industry Overview

Boston Beer Company and the Lion Brewery both compete in the craft beer segment of the U.S. brewing industry. Boston Beer estimates that this segment of the market accounted for approximately 4.7 million barrels of beer in 1996. While the total U.S. beer industry shipments over the last five years have remained relatively level, the craft beer segment has grown at an average compound annual rate of 39% from 1991 to 1996. The primary cause for this growth is increased consumer demand for traditional, full-flavored beers, such as craft brews and those produced by microbreweries. Craft brews are produced by contract brewers, small regional brewers and brewpubs as well at the major U.S. brewers. Craft beers are generally brewed with higher quality hops, malted barley, yeast and water, without adjuncts such as rice, corn or stabilizers.

There are very few barriers to entry to this industry and consequently there has been a flood of new entrants. These tend to be smaller companies that do not have the financial or logistical (e.g., distribution networks) strength of the "big three" U.S. brewers (Anheiser Busch, Adolph Coors, and Philip Morris). As market share for craft beer has been taken away from the big three, they have responded with bands of their own. Competition is fierce and most analysts believe that there will be a shakeout in the industry. Smaller brewers will go out of business, combine with other craft brewers, or be purchased by the big three.

Company Overviews

Boston Beer

The Boston Beer Company is the largest craft brewer by volume in the U.S and is located in Boston, Massachusetts. In fiscal 1996, the Company sold 1,213,000 barrels of beer, more than the next five largest craft brewers combined. The Company was founded in 1984 and over the last five years, the Company's net sales have grown from $29.5 million to $191.1 million, representing a compound annual growth rate of 46%. From 1995 to 1996, the Company's net sales grew by 26%.

Boston Beer Company has adopted a strategy of creating and marketing a wide variety of high-quality, full-flavored beers throughout the U.S., Canada, Sweden, Germany, Hong Kong, and the United Kingdom. The Company distributes its beers through a network of over 400 independent distributors throughout the U.S. The Company's marketing strategy consists of efforts to increase sales through new product introductions and substantial trade and consumer awareness programs. These endeavors are supported by a large, well-trained and rapidly expanding field-sales organization. In addition, the Company has historically engaged in extensive media campaigns, primarily radio advertising. The Company has also dedicated itself to developing new products and plans to remain a leading innovator in the craft beer industry. As of 1996, the Company offered 18 separate craft beers, most of which are centered around the Samuel Adams product line. They believe their premium pricing strategy, along with their extensive distribution system, has allowed them to develop strong relationships with distributors, retailers and consumers.

Boston Beer Company has adopted a "contract brewing" strategy, outsourcing the brewing process to other breweries which have excess capacity. Currently, the Company utilizes five main breweries that collectively account for the majority of the Company's production. Only a small portion of the Company's production is produced at the Company's Boston brewery. Boston Beer believes that this strategy gives it flexibility as well as quality and cost advantages over its competitors. By brewing in multiple locations, the Company believes that it can reduce its distribution costs and deliver fresher beer to consumers. Generally, the Company is charged a per unit rate for brewing, fermenting and packaging, as well as the cost of the raw materials.

Lion Brewery

The Lion Brewery is a producer and bottler of brewed beverages, including malta, specialty beers, and soft drinks. The company was incorporated in Pennsylvania in 1933 and has current production of approximately 340,000 barrels. The company is currently in the process of increasing production to approximately 400,000 barrels. The Company is the dominant producer of malta in the continental United States. The Company brews craft beers both for sale under its own label and on a contract basis.

The Lion Brewery's current business strategy is to enhance its position as a leading producer of specialty brewed beverages by rapidly expanding production and marketing of craft beers and other malt-based premium products while maintaining the growth of its nonalcoholic brewed beverages. One of the key elements of this strategy is to continue to produce a variety of high-quality, full-flavored beverages. To monitor the control of the brewing process, the Company maintains its own quality control laboratory in Pennsylvania. The Company intends to continue to produce in its company-owned and operated facilities. The Company feels that this strategy will allow them to optimize the quality and consistency of its products, to achieve the greatest control over its production costs and to formulate new brewed products.

The Company currently distributes craft beers under its own labels through a network of wholesale distributor relationships in twelve states, with the majority of sales concentrated in Pennsylvania. The Company is also committed to developing and introducing new products to appeal to the strong consumer interest in full-flavored craft beers.

The Company brews many distinctive craft beers and other specialty malt beverages under contract for other labels. Some of these customers are microbreweries and brewpubs that need additional brewing capacity to meet their production requirements. The Company typically uses the contractor's own recipe, or in other circumstances, the Company will assist in formulating beer and specialty malt beverages for customers marketing their own labels. The Lion Brewery craft beer and specialty malt beverages produced for sale under its own labels and under contract for others accounted for approximately 19% and 12% of net sales in fiscal 1996 and 1995, respectively.

In 1996, Lion Brewery's malta sales accounted for 67.8% of net sales. Craft beers and popularly priced beers accounted for 22.8% of net sales and specialty soft drinks accounted for 9.4% of net sales. Over the past three years, craft beer sales as a percentage of net sales have increased from 7.9% to 19.1%, while popularly priced beers have decreased from 6.8% to 3.7%. Malta sales, as a percentage of net sales, have decreased over the last three years from 78.6% to 67.8%, while specialty soft drinks have increased from 6.7% to 9.4% of total net sales. The Company's current marketing strategy is to increase its penetration into existing markets while expanding to other markets simultaneously. The Company anticipates significantly increasing its sales and marketing efforts by hiring additional sales personnel and increasing public brand name exposure through print, outdoor and electronic advertising on a selective basis.

In 1996, the company recapitalized itself by issuing stock and using the proceeds to repay its long-term debt.

Intercompany Differences

There are several important differences between Boston and Lion. First, Boston is a much larger company and they sell their product (craft beer) nationally. Lion sells its product regionally. In addition, Lion is not solely a craft brewer. They produce cheap beer for others, soft drinks, and malta a non-alcoholic brewed beverage popular in Hispanic markets. Indeed, malta is the company's major product. Over the past few years Lion has tried to change its sales mix to focus on more profitable products. These products compete in an increasingly competitive environment. Another important difference is that Boston brews very little of the beer it sells itself. Rather it uses the excess capacity of other brewers on a "contract" basis. Lion brews its own product. These differences should be reflected in the financials of the two companies. For example, we should expect gross margins to be higher at Boston than Lion because of the different sales mixes. We should expect higher asset turnover at Boston than Lion because Boston is not saddled with fixed assets. Because Lion owns is own property, plant and equipment, they are more likely to have a greater proportion of long-term debt than Boston.

Accounting Issues

Audit Reports

Both companies received clean audit opinions from their auditors (Boston used Coopers and Lybrand, Lion used Arthur Andersen). Although the audit opinion is not a seal of approval when it comes to investing, we can be confident that the financial statements were prepared in accordance with GAAP and that they are materially correct.

Differences in GAAP

Both companies use U.S. GAAP. There were no major changes in the methods chosen (over time) and both companies appear to use the same methods. Estimates of useful lives are within normal ranges for both companies. Both use FIFO to value inventories. Both companies provide "pro-forma" income tax data. They do so as a result of various corporate reorganizations that were conducted prior to becoming public companies. We use those pro-forma figures in the analyses that follow.

Off-B/S items

Both companies use operating leases which raises the question of whether there are off-balance sheet obligations and assets. At Boston the undiscounted amount of future lease payments is $3,273, an amount not likely viewed as material in relation to the balance sheet (especially in light of the lack of other long-term debt). At Lion, the corresponding figure is $905. Although as a proportion of total reported liabilities the amount is significant, we have not adjusted long-term debt or assets on the grounds that conclusions about the overall leverage of the company would be unaffected (the company currently has a total debt to equity ratio of about (3/12 =) .25; adding the additional lease payments (even undiscounted) would lead to a ratio of less than .33).

Other Adjustments

No other significant accounting adjustments were deemed necessary. As a starting point in our analysis, we use ending figures from the balance sheets to calculate the ratios. Were we to go into more detail, we could use balance sheet averages. This would limit the number of years we could analyze for Boston and Lion as they do not report more than two balance sheets. Note that the Lion figures exclude the extraordinary item and warrant accruals on the grounds that neither is recurring. The Boston figures are based on the pro-forma figures for income taxes.

ROE

We start our analysis with the DuPont ROE framework. This provides us with an overview of overall profitability (from an owner's perspective) and also provides an initial decomposition of ROE. Our more detailed analyses will probe deeper into reasons for differences in ROE across the two companies and over time. Note that U.S. industrial firms have on average earned ROEs of 12-14% in the long run. When firms are earning above or below that range we ought to ask ourselves why. Is there a need for a change in strategy? Of managers? A redeployment of capital? Does the company have sustainable barriers to entry? Will the high ROE attract competitors? What steps are being taken to deal with that competition? And so on.

DuPont Results

Boston Beer

		1996	1995
ROE	Net Income (pro forma in 1995)	8,385,000	5,896,000
	Common Shareholders' Equity	64,831,000	54,798,000
=		**12.9%**	**10.8%**
Taxes	NI	8,385,000	5,896,000
	EBT	14,871,000	10,379,000
=		**56.4%**	**56.8%**
Debt Cost	EBT	14,871,000	10,379,000
	EBIT	13,157,000	9,420,000
=		**113.0%**	**110.2%**
Return on Sales	EBIT	13,157,000	9,420,000
	Sales	191,116,000	151,313,000
=		**6.9%**	**6.2%**
Asset Turns	Sales	191,116,000	151,313,000
	Assets	96,553,000	76,690,000
=		**1.98**	**1.97**
Leverage	Assets	96,553,000	76,690,000
	Common Shareholders' Equity	64,831,000	54,708,000
=		**1.49**	**1.40**

Lion Brewery

		1996	1995
ROE	Net Income (before extraordinary and warrants)	1,418,000	1,051,000
	Common Shareholders' Equity	12,620,000	2,317,000
=		**11.2%**	**45.4%**
Taxes	NI	1,418,000	1,051,000
	EBT	2,543,000	1,972,000
=		**55.8%**	**53.3%**
Debt Cost	EBT	2,543,000	1,972,000
	EBIT	3,063,000	3,014,000
=		**83.0%**	**65.4%**
Return on Sales	EBIT	3,063,000	3,014,000
	Sales	26,439,000	24,793,000
=		**11.6%**	**12.2%**
Asset Turns	Sales	26,439,000	24,793,000
	Assets	15,954,000	14,441,000
=		**1.66**	**1.72**
Leverage	Assets	15,954,000	14,441,000
	Common Shareholders' Equity	12,620,000	2,317,000
=		**1.26**	**6.23**

The major insights we gain from the ROE analysis are as follows:

- Neither company is earning an extraordinarily high ROE. At 12.9% ROE Boston is outpacing Lion at 11.2%.

- More significant is the trend in ROE. Boston's is on the rise, Lion's on a steep decline.

- The major reason for Lion's decline in ROE is the decline in leverage. Assets/CSE has dropped from 6.23 to 1.26 as a result of the recapitalization of the company in 1996. That is, they issued $9,466,000 of new shares and used the proceeds to repay $7,584,000 of long-term debt and 721,000 of line-of-credit.

- Offsetting the reduction in leverage at Lion is the increase in the proportion of pre-interest profit retained by the owners. That is, EBT/EBIT has increased from 65.4% to 83.0% in 1996. At Boston, the figure is greater than 100% because they have net interest income (versus net expense). They are sitting on over $35 million in marketable securities as a result of their recent IPO. They indicate in their annual report that they will be using some of that to purchase a new manufacturing facility in Cincinnati. This is a departure from their current "contract brewing" strategy, and should be monitored.

- Boston Beer has done a better job managing its tax costs. They keep an average of 56.4 cents per dollar of pretax earnings versus 55.8 cents at Lion. Lion, however, is improving in this area and Boston actually declined from 56.8 cents in 1995.

- Although Boston is the name brand firm, their operating return on sales is only 6.9% in 1996 (up from 6.2% in 1995) versus a much higher 11.6% at Lion (down from 12.2% in 1995). We will explore the reasons for this difference and speculate on future trends in a later section.

- Boston Beer's asset utilization exceeded Lion's in both 1995 and 1996. This is to be expected given Boston's contract brewing strategy (other things equal, they will have less assets as they don't own their own manufacturing facilities). But as we indicated above, that might change with Boston's planned purchase of new facilities.

Common-size I/S—Profitability

Boston Beer

	1996/12/28	1995/12/28	1994/12/28	1996	1995	1994
Sales	$213,879,000	$169,362,000	$128,077,000	111.9%	111.9%	111.5%
Less excise taxes	$22,763,000	$18,049,000	$13,244,000	11.9%	11.9%	11.5%
Net sales	*$191,116,000*	*$151,313,000*	*$114,833,000*	*100.0%*	*100.0%*	*100.0%*
Cost of sales	$95,786,000	$73,847,000	$52,851,000	50.1%	48.8%	46.0%
Gross profit	*$95,330,000*	*$77,466,000*	*$61,982,000*	*49.9%*	*51.2%*	*54.0%*
Operating expenses:						
Advertising, promotional and selling expenses	$70,131,000	$60,461,000	$46,503,000	36.7%	40.0%	40.5%
General and administrative expenses	$12,042,000	$7,585,000	$6,593,000	6.3%	5.0%	5.7%
Total operating expenses	$82,173,000	$68,046,000	$53,096,000	43.0%	45.0%	46.2%
Operating Income	*$13,157,000*	*$9,420,000*	*$8,886,000*	*6.9%*	*6.2%*	*7.7%*
Other income (expense):						
Interest income	$1,932,000	$452,000	$429,000	1.0%	0.3%	0.4%
Interest expense	($236,000)	($250,000)	($233,000)	-0.1%	-0.2%	-0.2%
Other income, net	$18,000	$757,000	$3,000	0.0%	0.5%	0.0%
Total other income	$1,714,000	$959,000	$199,000	0.9%	0.6%	0.2%
Income before income taxes	*$14,871,000*	*$10,379,000*	*$9,085,000*	*7.8%*	*6.9%*	*7.9%*
Provision (benefit) for income taxes	$6,486,000	($2,195,000)	$0	3.4%	-1.5%	0.0%
Net income	$8,385,000	$12,574,000	$9,085,000	4.4%	8.3%	7.9%
Pro forma data (unaudited) (Note B):						
Income before pro forma income taxes		$10,379,000	$9,085,000		6.9%	7.9%
Pro forma income tax expense		$4,483,000	$3,765,000		3.0%	3.3%
Pro forma net income		**$5,896,000**	**$5,320,000**		3.9%	4.6%

Lion Brewery

	1996/09/30	1995/09/30	1996	1995
Gross sales	$26,983,000	$25,175,000	102.1%	101.5%
Less excise taxes	$544,000	$382,000	2.1%	1.5%
Net sales	*$26,439,000*	*$24,793,000*	*100.0%*	*100.0%*
Cost of sales	$19,939,000	$18,834,000	75.4%	76.0%
Gross profit	*$6,500,000*	*$5,959,000*	*24.6%*	*24.0%*
Operating expenses:				
Delivery	$824,000	$827,000	3.1%	3.3%
Selling, advertising and promotional expenses	$1,240,000	$782,000	4.7%	3.2%
General and administrative	$1,373,000	$1,336,000	5.2%	5.4%
	$3,437,000	$2,945,000	13.0%	11.9%
Operating income	*$3,063,000*	*$3,014,000*	*11.6%*	*12.2%*
Interest expense and amortization of debt discount, net	$520,000	$1,042,000	2.0%	4.2%
Income before provision for income taxes and extraordinary item	*$2,543,000*	*$1,972,000*	*9.6%*	*8.0%*
Provision for income taxes	$1,125,000	$921,000	4.3%	3.7%
Income before extraordinary item	*$1,418,000*	*$1,051,000*	*5.4%*	*4.2%*
Extraordinary item, net of income tax benefit of $228,000	($322,000)	($0)	-1.2%	0.0%
Net income	*$1,096,000*	*$1,051,000*	*4.1%*	*4.2%*
Warrant accretion	$89,000	$300,000	0.3%	1.2%
Net income available to common shareholders	$1,007,000	$751,000	3.8%	3.0%

Boston Beer: Return on Sales

	1996	1995	
Gross Margin	49.9%	51.2%	
SGA as % of sales	6.3%	5.0%	
Advertising as % of sales	36.7%	40.0%	
Operating Return on sales	6.9%	6.2%	Uses EBIT
Net Return on sales	4.4%	3.9%	Uses net income

Boston's return on sales increased in 1996. Looking at the common size income statement we see that the improvement was the result of offsetting improvements and pressures. Reflecting the increased competitive pressure in the craft brewing industry, Boston's gross margin percent dropped 1.3% points to 49.9%. In addition, SG&A increased in 1996 by 1.3%. This was offset by a reduction in the cost of advertising as a percent of sales (36.7% vs. 40.0% in 1995). This decrease seems odd given the company's strategy of creating a solid brand name through advertising. Nonetheless, we see that total advertising dollars increased by $10,000,000 suggesting that the decrease in advertising as a percent of sales was due to efficiencies of scale and not a cutback in promotion of the brand.

Lion Brewery: Return on Sales

	1996	1995	
Gross Margin	24.6%	24.0%	
SGA as % of sales	5.2%	5.4%	
Advertising as % of sales	4.7%	3.2%	
Operating Return on sales	11.6%	12.2%	Uses EBIT
Net Return on sales	5.4%	4.2%	Uses net income

Lion Brewery's net return on sales also increased in 1996 (4.2% to 5.4%) despite a decrease in operating ROS (12.2% to 11.6%). The company was able to increase its gross margin as a percent of sales even though the competitive landscape was not friendly. They achieved the improvement via a change in sales mix (i.e., a more profitable mix of craft beers and beer brewed under contract for others). SG&A was held in check, a good sign. Furthermore, consistent with the company's move to establish a premium brand in its markets, we see an increase in advertising as a percent of sales (up 1.5% to 4.7% in 1996). In dollar terms, the company's advertising costs are tiny compared with Boston Beer's. Although the operating ROS declined, the drop was more than offset by reduced interest costs (2.0% of sales versus 4.2% in 1995) and better income tax management (see later sections).

Overall, Lion is generating a better return on sales than is Boston. Although Boston starts with a considerably higher gross margin percent (49.9% versus 24.6%), Lion has a better operating return on sales (11.6% vs. 6.9% in 1996). Lion's operating ROS has declined slightly while Boston's has improved from 1995 to 1996. Although Boston has particularly high gross margins, their advertising costs offset that advantage over Lion. If Boston can leverage efficiency of scale in advertising (and further reduce advertising as a percent of sales) they may be able to take the lead in ROS.

For comparison purposes, the table that follows provides data from other companies in the industry. Lion and Boston are neither leaders nor laggards in the industry.

Gross Margin

Industry Data from PricewaterhouseCoopers EDGARScan

(note that the industry data has not been adjusted for proforma taxes or other unusual items)

	1996	1995	1994
BOSTON BEER CO INC	49.9%	51.2%	
LION BREWERY INC	24.6%	24.0%	
ANHEUSER BUSCH COMPANIES INC	36.0%	34.3%	35.2%
COORS ADOLPH CO	46.8%	46.7%	47.8%
REDHOOK ALE BREWERY INC	33.9%	34.5%	41.8%
PETES BREWING CO	50.8%		

EBIT Margin

	1996	1995	1994
BOSTON BEER CO INC	7.9%	7.0%	
LION BREWERY INC	11.6%	12.2%	
ANHEUSER BUSCH COMPANIES INC	19.1%	16.3%	18.9%
COORS ADOLPH CO	4.2%	4.1%	5.7%
REDHOOK ALE BREWERY INC	13.6%	19.3%	23.1%
PETES BREWING CO	3.5%		

Net Return on Sales

	1996	1995	1994
BOSTON BEER CO INC	4.4%	8.3%	
LION BREWERY INC	5.4%	4.2%	
ANHEUSER BUSCH COMPANIES INC	10.9%	6.2%	10.3%
COORS ADOLPH CO	2.0%	2.1%	2.8%
REDHOOK ALE BREWERY INC	8.6%	12.3%	14.2%
PETES BREWING CO	2.4%		

Asset Utilization—Turnovers

Boston Beer: Asset Turns

	1996	1995	
A/R Turnover	11.8	9.4	uses ending AR
Average Collection Period	30.9	38.8	
Inventory Turnover	7.4	8.0	uses ending inventory
Average Holding Period	49.5	45.9	
A/P Turnover	5.6	N/A	uses purchases
Average Payment Period	65.2	N/A	
A/P Turnover	5.4	7.5	uses COGS
Average Payment Period	67.8	48.4	
Conversion Cycle in days	15.2	N/A	uses purchases
Conversion Cycle in days	12.7	36.3	uses COGS
Plant Asset Turnover	14.6	27.5	
Allowance for Doubtful Accounts as a percent of Gross A/R	-0.11	-0.01	
Allowance for Doubtful Accounts as a percent of sales	-0.01	0.00	

Lion Brewery: Asset Turns

	1996	1995	
A/R Turnover	13.2	10.0	uses ending AR
Average Collection Period	27.6	36.5	
Inventory Turnover	9.4	9.4	uses ending inventory
Average Holding Period	39.0	38.8	
A/P Turnover	12.1	N/A	uses purchases
Average Payment Period	30.3	N/A	
A/P Turnover	12.0	9.5	uses COGS
Average Payment Period	30.4	38.3	
Conversion Cycle in days	36.3	N/A	uses purchases
Conversion Cycle in days	36.1	36.9	uses COGS
Plant Asset Turnover	7.5	7.7	
Allowance for Doubtful Accounts as a percent of Gross A/R	-0.07	-0.05	
Allowance for Doubtful Accounts as a percent of sales	-0.01	-0.01	

As we might expect given Boston's contract brewing strategy, their overall asset turnover is higher than Lion's. At first glance, the difference is not especially large (1.98 times versus 1.66 times in 1996). However, we need to consider the temporary excess cash and marketable securities on Boston's balance sheet. If Boston reduced its cash as a percent of assets to the same level as Lion (approximately 13% of total assets), then its total asset turnover would be 2.8 times, a significant increase. This ratio should be monitored in the future. Note, also, that Boston's plant asset turnover (at 14.6 times in 1996) is twice that of Lion (at 7.5 times in 1996). The turnover has dropped at Boston from 27.5 times in 1995 mainly due to a significant purchase of plant and equipment in 1996 (again, the effect of departing from the pure contract brewing strategy).

Both companies appear to be managing their receivables well, with average collection periods in the 30-day range and improved over 1995 figures. Lion manages to produce and sell its inventory more quickly than Boston (39 days vs. 49 days). Boston's inventory holding period is on the rise and needs to be monitored. What is causing the increase? Is inventory (of perishable product) increasing? A look at the details of their inventory is helpful in understanding the increase. The bulk of the increase in Boston's inventory is in raw materials. That suggests that the company is gearing up for increased sales and not that it has a problem with unwanted finished goods.

We can estimate the time each company takes to pay its obligations by looking at the ratio of Purchases to Payables and dividing it into 365 days. Unfortunately there are insufficient data to calculate this ratio for more than one year. Consequently, we estimate the payment period using COGS instead of Purchases. Doing so, we observe that Boston is paying its obligations much later than Lion (approximately 67 days versus 30 days). Given the large balance in cash and marketable securities that Boston has, this seems odd. It may be that inventory purchases towards the end of the year are skewing the ratio (i.e., that the payables balance is abnormally high due to the timing of a purchase). That may also explain the increase in inventory. These are both worth looking into.

The conversion cycle is measured as the sum of average inventory holding period and average collection period less the average payment period. It measures the net time that a company has to finance its operations. That is, it buys and holds/produces inventory for x days and then sells it and waits y days to be paid. Cash is tied up in the process. One way to finance that is to delay payments to suppliers. The open period needs to be financed somehow. The shorter the period the better. At Boston, the conversion cycle (inventory to cash) improved from 36.3 days to 12.7 days in 1996. The corresponding figures at Lion are 36.9 and 36.1 days. Boston is more effective at turning inventory into cash.

Industry Data from PricewaterhouseCoopers EDGARScan
(note that the industry data has not been adjusted for proforma taxes or other unusual items)

Total Asset Turnover	1996	1995	1994
BOSTON BEER CO INC	1.98	1.97	
LION BREWERY INC	1.66	1.72	
ANHEUSER BUSCH COMPANIES INC	1.04	0.98	0.95
COORS ADOLPH CO	1.56	1.50	1.49
REDHOOK ALE BREWERY INC	0.38	0.30	
PETES BREWING CO	1.07		

Collection Period (Days)	1996	1995	1994
BOSTON BEER CO INC	34.6	39.2	
LION BREWERY INC	27.6	36.5	
ANHEUSER BUSCH COMPANIES INC	21.3	19.2	21.8
COORS ADOLPH CO	19.7	20.5	19.0
REDHOOK ALE BREWERY INC	21.0	28.6	
PETES BREWING CO	39.6		

Inventory Days COGS	1996	1995	1994
BOSTON BEER CO INC	49.5	45.9	
LION BREWERY INC	39.0	38.8	
ANHEUSER BUSCH COMPANIES INC	27.8	31.3	29.8
COORS ADOLPH CO	39.2	46.0	48.4
REDHOOK ALE BREWERY INC	34.5	28.8	
PETES BREWING CO	46.5		

Accounts Payables Days COGS	1996	1995	1994
BOSTON BEER CO INC	67.8	48.4	
LION BREWERY INC	15.4	38.3	
ANHEUSER BUSCH COMPANIES INC	38.1	36.7	42.5
COORS ADOLPH CO			56.2
REDHOOK ALE BREWERY INC	63.1	103.9	
PETES BREWING CO	55.6		

Boston Beer: Leverage

	1996	1995	
Debt to Equity	48.9%	40.0%	uses total liabilities
Long-term Debt to Equity	2.8%	3.4%	uses LTD only
Current Ratio	2.60	3.26	
Quick Ratio	1.91	2.63	

Lion Brewery: Leverage

	1996	1995	
Debt to Equity	26.4%	492.1%	uses total liabilities
Long-term Debt to Equity	0.0%	264.6%	uses LTD only
Current Ratio	2.19	1.01	
Quick Ratio	1.38	0.53	

Both companies have very little in the way of long-term debt on their balance sheets. Lion had a substantial amount in 1995 but paid it off via the proceeds of a share issuance in 1996. Most of the liabilities at Boston Beer are current. Their strong current and quick ratios indicate that repaying the debt should not pose a problem. Although Lion's current and quick ratios are somewhat weaker than Boston's, they remain strong.

Debt/Equity ratio	1996	1995	1994
BOSTON BEER CO INC	9.33	9.90	
LION BREWERY INC	0.00	414.53	
ANHEUSER BUSCH COMPANIES INC	4.63	9.42	8.92
COORS ADOLPH CO	19.32	23.08	17.35
REDHOOK ALE BREWERY INC	164.55	50.68	
PETES BREWING CO			

Current Ratio	1996	1995	1994
BOSTON BEER CO INC	2.60	3.26	
LION BREWERY INC	2.19	1.01	
ANHEUSER BUSCH COMPANIES INC	1.02	1.22	1.04
COORS ADOLPH CO	1.42	1.11	0.93
REDHOOK ALE BREWERY INC	1.13	4.08	
PETES BREWING CO	3.95	9.50	

BOSTON BEER CO INC

	1996/12/28	1995/12/28	1996/12/28	1995/12/28
ASSETS				
Current Assets:				
Cash & cash equivalents	$5,060,000	$1,877,000	5.2%	2.4%
Short term investments	$35,926,000	$34,730,000	37.2%	45.3%
Accounts receivable, gross	$18,109,000	$16,265,000	18.8%	21.2%
Allowance for doubtful accounts	($1,930,000)	($175,000)	-2.0%	-0.2%
Accounts receivable, net	$16,179,000	$16,090,000	16.8%	21.0%
Inventories	$13,002,000	$9,280,000	13.5%	12.1%
Prepaid expenses	$674,000	$437,000	0.7%	0.6%
Deferred income taxes	$2,968,000	$1,011,000	3.1%	1.3%
Other current assets	$3,882,000	$1,858,000	4.0%	2.4%
Total current assets	*$77,691,000*	*$65,283,000*	*80.5%*	*85.1%*
Restricted investments	$611,000	$602,000	0.6%	0.8%
Equipment and leasehold improvements, at cost	$21,043,000	$9,690,000	21.8%	12.6%
Accumulated depreciation	($6,412,000)	($3,531,000)	-6.6%	-4.6%
PPE, Net	$14,631,000	$6,159,000	15.2%	8.0%
Deferred income taxes	$151,000	$1,777,000	0.2%	2.3%
Other assets	$3,469,000	$2,869,000	3.6%	3.7%
Total assets	**$96,553,000**	**$76,690,000**	**100.0%**	**100.0%**
LIABILITIES AND STOCKHOLDERS' EQUITY				
Current Liabilities:				
Accounts payable	$17,783,000	$9,793,000	18.4%	12.8%
Accrued expenses	$12,064,000	$10,149,000	12.5%	13.2%
Current maturities of long-term debt	$75,000	$75,000	0.1%	0.1%
Total current liabilities	*$29,922,000*	*$20,017,000*	*31.0%*	*26.1%*
Long-term debt, less current maturities	$1,800,000	$1,875,000	1.9%	2.4%
Total Liabilities	*$31,722,000*	*$21,892,000*	*32.9%*	*28.5%*
Commitments and Contingencies (Note I)				
Stockholders' Equity:				
Class A Common Stock, $.01 par value; 20,300,000 shares authorized; 15,972,058, and 15,643,664 issued and outstanding as of December 28, 1996 and December 31, 1995, respectively	$160,000	$156,000	0.2%	0.2%
Class B Common Stock, $.01 par value; 4,200,000 shares authorized; 4,107,355 issued and outstanding as of December 28, 1996 and December 31, 1995, respectively	$41,000	$41,000	0.0%	0.1%
Additional paid-in-capital	$55,391,000	$53,482,000	57.4%	69.7%
Unearned compensation	($363,000)	($509,000)	-0.4%	-0.7%
Unrealized loss on Investments in marketable securities	($442,000)	$0	-0.5%	0.0%
Unrealized gain on forward exchange contract	$31,000	$0	0.0%	0.0%
Retained earnings	$10,013,000	$1,628,000	10.4%	2.1%
Total stockholders' equity	*$64,831,000*	*$54,798,000*	*67.1%*	*71.5%*
Total liabilities and stockholders' equity	**$96,553,000**	**$76,690,000**	**100.0%**	**100.0%**

LION BREWERY INC

	1996/09/30	1995/09/30	1996/09/30	1995/09/30
Current assets:				
Cash and cash equivalents	$1,992,000	$0	12.5%	0.0%
Accounts receivable	$2,158,000	$2,605,000	13.5%	18.0%
Allowance for doubtful accounts	($157,000)	($129,000)	-1.0%	-0.9%
Accounts Receivable, net	$2,001,000	$2,476,000	12.5%	17.1%
Inventories	$2,128,000	$2,003,000	13.3%	13.9%
Prepaid expenses and other assets	$190,000	$277,000	1.2%	1.9%
Total current assets	*$6,311,000*	*$4,756,000*	*39.6%*	*32.9%*
Property, plant & equipment, gross	$5,284,000	$4,376,000	33.1%	30.3%
Accumulated depreciation	($1,684,000)	($1,122,000)	-10.6%	-7.8%
Property, plant & equipment, net	$3,600,000	$3,254,000	22.6%	22.5%
Goodwill, net of accumulated amortization of $475,000 and $311,000 at September 30, 1996 and 1995, respectively	$6,039,000	$6,203,000	37.9%	43.0%
Deferred financing costs and other assets, net of accumulated amortization of $144,000 at September 30, 1995	$4,000	$228,000	0.0%	1.6%
	$15,954,000	$14,441,000	100.0%	100.0%
LIABILITIES AND SHAREHOLDERS' EQUITY				
Current liabilities:				
Current portion of long-term debt	$0	$1,745,000	0.0%	12.1%
Accounts payable	$1,663,000	$1,978,000	10.4%	13.7%
Accrued expenses	$839,000	$478,000	5.3%	3.3%
Refundable deposits	$205,000	$171,000	1.3%	1.2%
Income taxes payable	$178,000	$330,000	1.1%	2.3%
Total current liabilities	*$2,885,000*	*$4,702,000*	*18.1%*	*32.6%*
Long-term debt, less current portion	$0	$6,131,000	0.0%	42.5%
Net pension liability	$243,000	$218,000	1.5%	1.5%
Deferred income taxes	$206,000	$351,000	1.3%	2.4%
Total liabilities	$3,334,000	$11,402,000	20.9%	79.0%
Warrants	$0	$722,000	0.0%	5.0%
Shareholders' equity:				
Common stock, $.01 par value; 10,000,000 shares authorized; 3,885,052 and 1,851,183 shares issued and outstanding at September 30, 1996 and 1995, respectively	$39,000	$19,000	0.2%	0.1%
Additional paid-in capital	$10,612,000	$1,304,000	66.5%	9.0%
Adjustment to reflect minimum pension liability, net of deferred income taxes	($42,000)	($10,000)	-0.3%	-0.1%
Retained earnings	$2,011,000	$1,004,000	12.6%	7.0%
Total shareholders' equity	*$12,620,000*	*$2,317,000*	*79.1%*	*16.0%*
Total liabilities and shareholders' equity	**$15,954,000**	**$14,441,000**	**100.0%**	**100.0%**

Boston Beer: Interest Cost

	1996	1995	
Average Interest Cost	-0.13	-0.13	uses ending LTD
Times Interest Earned	-55.75	-37.68	

Lion Brewery: Interest Cost

	1996	1995	
Average Interest Cost	0	0.17	uses ending LTD
Times Interest Earned	5.9	2.9	

Because neither company uses much long-term debt, very little interest expense is incurred. In fact Boston has net interest income in both 1995 and 1995. Both companies have healthy Times-interest-earned ratios, too.

Taxes

Boston Beer: Tax Costs

	1996	1995	
Average Tax Rate	43.6%	43.2%	

Lion Brewery: Tax Costs

	1996	1995	
Average Tax Rate	44.2%	46.7%	

Both Boston Beer and Lion Brewery have 'normal' tax rates. From the details in the notes to the financial statements, we find that (based on the proforma figures), both companies tax rates exceed the U.S. statutory corporate rate of 35% due mainly to the effect of state taxes. Both companies report mainly current income tax expense (i.e., the deferred component is relatively small). This suggests that book and tax incomes are similar—an indication that accounting income may not be aggressive. (When there are large book-tax differences that result in relatively small amounts of current tax expense, it may be a signal that management has taken liberties with its accounting accruals—delaying expenses and recording revenue early for accounting but not for tax purposes.)

Boston Beer: Cash Flows

	1996	1995	1994
Net income	$8,385,000	$12,574,000	$9,085,000
Net cash provided by **operating** activities:	$15,763,000	$2,440,000	$13,290,000
Net cash used in **investing**	($13,002,000)	($31,247,000)	($5,271,000)
Net cash provided by (used for) **financing** activities	$422,000	$30,586,000	$11,669,000
Net increase (decrease) in cash and cash equivalents	$3,183,000	$1,779,000	($3,650,000)
Cash and cash equivalents at beginning of period	$1,877,000	$98,000	$3,748,000
Cash and cash equivalents at end of period	$5,060,000	$1,877,000	$98,000

Boston Beer has a very healthy cash position at the end of 1996. In addition, the company has a large portfolio of marketable securities—another liquid asset. In 1994 and 1996 operating cash flows were significantly greater than net income. Some analysts consider this a signal of good earnings quality. If aggressive accounting for revenues and expenses was taking place, one would expect earnings to be greater than operating cash flow. Major reasons for the difference in 1994 and 1996 are the depreciation addback and the company's use of accounts payable and accrued expenses to fund its increased receivables and inventories. That is, the increase in payables and accrued expenses more than offset the increase in receivables and inventory. In 1995, when operating cash flow was significantly lower than net income, the major reason was that the increase in payables and accrued expenses did not keep pace with the increase in receivables, inventory, deferred taxes and other assets. Given that pattern, one might predict that operating cash flow in 1997 might be lower than net income.

Operating cash flows have been sufficient to cover investing cash outflows in 1994 and 1996. 1995 shows a significant deficiency, but that is misleading. The bulk of the 1995 investing outflows were purchases of marketable securities. These optional outflows are not dependent on operating cash flow. Indeed the reason for the major purchase of marketable securities in 1995 was the company's IPO proceeds.

In 1995 the company issued almost $50 million of common stock in an initial public offering. Over $19 million of that was used to pay off the original partners. The remainder has been used mainly to invest in marketable securities. The company has indicated that it has plans to purchase manufacturing facilities and expand its operations. Given its significant cash position, it appears to be in a position to do so.

Lion Brewery: Cash Flows

	1996	1995
Net income	$1,096,000	$1,051,000
Net cash provided by **operating** activities	$2,689,000	$2,475,000
Net cash used in **investing** activities	($908,000)	($307,000)
Net cash provided by (used in) **financing** activities	$211,000	($2,309,000)
Net increase (decrease) in cash and cash equivalents	$1,992,000	($141,000)
Cash and cash equivalents. beginning of year	$0	$141,000
Cash and cash equivalents, end of year	$1,992,000	$0

Cash flow at Lion Brewery is healthy. The company generated positive operating cash flow in each of 1995 and 1996. Operating cash flow exceeded net income by a healthy amount, largely due to the addback of depreciation and amortization. In 1996, a $450,000 adjustment to net income due to the reduction in accounts receivable also added to operating cash flow.

Operating cash flow was sufficient to cover net investing needs in both years. Investing cash outflows were for the purchase of fixed assets.

Financing cash flows were net positive in 1996 and negative in 1995. The major activity in the financing area has been the company's reduction in long-term debt. In 1996, over $9 million dollars were raised and used to repay long-term debt. The remaining cash will be used for expansion and new equipment. The company has a line of credit available to it should additional cash needs arise.

Conclusion

Boston Beer and Lion Brewery are both in good financial shape at the end of 1996. They are both profitable (but with ROEs in the 12% range, they are not earning supernormal profits). Neither appears to be likely to run into liquidity or solvency problems. We identified operating differences across the firms. If each was able to achieve the other's efficiency levels in individual areas, profitability would be improved (e.g., if Boston were able to reduce SG&A as a percent of sales to the level achieved by Lion or if Lion was able to reduce its tax rate to Boston's level).

Their success in the future depends on how the intense competition in the craft brewing industry plays out. There is an increasing threat from the big three brewers and new entrants to the industry are popping up monthly. The squeeze on gross margins is already being felt by Boston. Lion is trying to enter a competitive market. Presently it does not have a national brand and it seems to be trying to find a niche. That is, it sells its own craft beer and malta, but it also sells soft drinks and low priced beer on a contract basis. Its strategy seems unfocused. Boston, on the other hand has established a national brand and may be able to weather the competitive storm better than some of its smaller and less well-capitalized competitors. Boston's IPO seems to have been well timed as they raised capital when the market for craft brewing companies was hot.

Both companies are betting on the continued trend in craft beer consumption. Although the market has expanded in recent years, it seems unlikely to topple the "regular" beer market in the U.S. Future success of both companies depends on how the trend plays out.

Of the two firms, Boston appears better positioned to succeed. In addition to its strong brand recognition, it has lots of liquidity, and is profitable without taking on a lot of leverage. The key to its continued success lies in its ability to continue to effectively use contract brewers and to expand its capacity to serve its customers. New products and effective marketing of the brand are, of course, critical as well.

Will we see supernormal profits from either of these firms in the future? It seems unlikely. The low barriers to entry and the tough competition arising from the big three brewers suggests that only normal profits will be earned. If the industry plays out like others that have had especially high ROE in the short run, we will see a shake out with weaker firms falling by the wayside in the near future. The competitive environment, combined with an overall industry "pie" that is not growing will ensure this!

Teaching Notes:

This case demonstrates product cost flow in a simple setting.

The T-accounts create a powerful visual representation of the cost and physical product flow. Set the T-accounts up on a chalkboard or an overhead with the following accounts (from left to right) accounts payable, raw materials, work-in-process, finished goods, cost of goods sold. Have the students fill in the T-accounts starting with opening and closing balances. The balancing entry in each account can be posted to the related (preceding) T-account to highlight the flow of costs.

Students may be confused by the labor charge of $50 million being posted to the inventory account. A discussion of labor, supplies, overhead, and other types of charges that would normally go through the WIP account is useful here.

Although the case does not require it, recreating the journal entries for each step will reinforce the concepts conveyed by the T-accounts.

a. Raw materials will include costs associated with the components of the Company's golf club inventory. Included in this amount will be shipping costs paid by Callaway to get the components to the manufacturing facility.

Work-in-process will include the cost of raw materials that have entered the manufacturing process. In addition, manufacturing salaries and an allocation of general factory costs will be included in the work-in-process balance.

Finished goods will include clubs that are completely ready for sale as well as any golf accessories that the Company sells such as shirts, caps, bags and other promotional material.

b. According to Note 3, inventories are net of an allowance for obsolescence. Adding back the allowance to the net inventory amounts results in gross inventory carrying values of $112,932,000 and $186,040,000 in 1999 and 1998, respectively.

c. The obsolete inventory allowance is most likely related to the raw materials and finished goods inventories. For example, Callaway likely holds inventories of graphite golf club shafts. If graphite technology changes prior to using up all the inventory, the company may have to write some of it down. Similarly, if golfers' tastes change in favor of mid-size club heads and the company is holding finished goods inventory that is primarily oversized heads, they may have to write down the cost of those items. (For the remainder of the case we assume that the obsolete inventory relates to finished goods.) As golf club assembly is not time consuming, there is little WIP inventory and there is not likely to be any obsolete inventory in that category.

d. There are two possibilities for the debit in this journal entry. Setting up an allowance (contra-asset) account is more sophisticated and is consistent with what Callaway actually does. Debiting the inventory account directly, while acceptable for this entry, obscures important information about the level of the obsolete inventory.

Dr.	Allowance for Obsolescence or Finished Goods	21,854	
Cr.	Cost of Goods Sold		21,854

To record a decrease in obsolete inventory.

It might seem odd that Callaway decreases (with the credit) the cost of goods sold for obsolete inventory. This happened because the company previously set up the provision for obsolete inventory. During the year, Callaway either (1) sold some of the marked-down inventory so that the need for the allowance at year end is reduced, or (2) determined that the previously marked down inventory could be sold at a higher price (again requiring a smaller allowance). In both cases, the adjustment goes to cost of goods sold.

The following examples illustrate what Callaway might have encountered in 1998 and 1999. Assume that at December 31, 1998 the company had $100,000 of inventory that it determined had a "market" value (per the lower of cost or market rules) of $63,152. In that case, they would need an allowance for obsolete inventory of $36,848 and would record it with the following adjusting journal entry (which assumes that no prior allowance existed).

| Dr. | Cost of Goods Sold (expense) | | 36,848 | |
| Cr. | Allowance for Obsolete Inventory | | | 36,848 |

To record a provision for obsolete inventory.

Assume further that at December 31, 1999 Callaway had still not sold the inventory but that the market value of the inventory was now $85,006. The allowance only needs to be $14,994 and so Callaway records the first entry (reversing a portion of the allowance).

Alternatively, Callaway might have sold all the obsolete inventory in 1999, but *other* inventory remaining at December 31 required an allowance of $14,994. When the initial obsolete inventory was sold, no adjustment to the allowance was made. At the end of the year, it is too high by $21,854 and so Callaway records the $21,854 reversal discussed previously.

e. The easiest way to determine purchases for raw materials (based on the problem's assumptions) is to work the T-accounts backward from cost of goods sold to finished goods through work-in-process to raw materials and finally to accounts payable.

There are several possible ways to deal with the obsolete inventory issue. One is to set up the finished goods-net, the other is to set up a separate T-account for the allowance. The former is easier and the solution below takes that approach.

Cost of Goods Sold

Beg. Bal.		0	
		21,854	Journal entry above
Transfer from fin. goods	398,259		
End Bal. I/S	376,405		

Finished Goods - Net of Obsolete Inventory

Beg. Bal.	45,020		
Journal entry above	21,854	398,259	COGS (I/S) (adjusted for obsolete inventory adjustment)
Transfer from WIP	382,052		
End Bal.	50,667		

Work-in-Process

Beg. Bal.	1,820		
Labor & Overhead	50,000	382,052	Transfer to Fin. Goods
Transfer from raw mat	331,635		
End Bal.	1,403		

Raw Materials

Beg. Bal.	102,352		
Purchases	275,151		
		331,635	Transfer to work in process
End Bal.	45,868		

Accounts Payable and Accrued Expenses

		10,341	Beg. Bal.
		275,151	Purchases of raw mat.
Cash Payments (plug)	274,195		
		11,297	End Bal.

e. i. The finished goods sold were transferred to the cost of goods sold account: $398,259.

e. ii. Finished goods transferred from work in process: $382,052.

e. iii. Raw materials transferred to work in process: $331,635.

e. iv. Raw materials purchased during the year: $275,151.

e. v. Cash disbursed during the year is the plug to the A/P account because of the assumption made in the question. Total disbursement was $274,195.

f. Inventory turnover is calculated by dividing cost of sales by the inventory.

	1999	1998
Cost of Sales	376,405	401,607
Inventory (net)		
1999	97,938	
1998		149,192
Inventory Turnover	3.84 times	2.69 times

g. Inventory holding period is calculated as 365 days/inventory turnover.

1999 365/3.84 = 95 days.
1998 365/2.69 = 136 days.

Despite the decrease in sales in 1999, Callaway is better managing its inventories (i.e., they are being sold more promptly).

h. Because the allowance is probably fully absorbed by the finished goods inventory, the percentage should be calculated on the gross amount of finished goods inventory. The obsolete portion of finished goods inventory was 23% and 45% in 1999 and 1998, respectively.

The reduction in the percentage of obsolete goods to total inventory could be the result of Callaway selling some of their obsolete goods during the year. Alternatively, Callaway may have been able to raise the price on some of its inventory, reducing the need for such a large allowance for obsolete inventory.

Note that Callaway went through a restructuring of their business in 1998 (see the income statement). This involved the disposal of significant inventories of books and golf-related items from businesses that Callaway golf decided to exit. The disposals took place in 1999.

Teaching Notes:

This case always generates class discussion. Students are amazed to learn how much discretion management has in capitalizing costs. Numerous articles about Chambers appeared in the financial press. Prior to the accounting scandal, Chambers was portrayed as a highly regarded growth firm. When the scandal broke, initial stories discussed the matching / conservatism tradeoff. By the end, however, it was clear that Chambers had hoodwinked the press, auditors, regulators, and investors—but only for a time.

Class discussion should emphasize how difficult it is to continue the practices Chambers engaged in. Discussion of how this could happen in an "efficient capital market" also is provocative and informative.

a. i. A cost is said to be incurred when an entity gives up assets or incurs a future commitment to give up assets in exchange for a good or service.

a. ii. Expenses, on the other hand, are decreases in net assets caused by the revenue-producing activities of an entity during a specific period. For example, a retail store that orders inventory in exchange for a promise to pay cash for the inventory in 30 days has incurred the cost of the inventory. However, no expense should be recognized until the inventory actually is sold to customers.

a. iii. The basic question is, "when will the cost generate revenues?" If the answer is, "sometime in the future" then one can argue that the cost should be capitalized because it meets the definition of an asset (expected future economic benefit). Otherwise the cost should be expensed.

a. iv. Capitalizing a cost does not mean that it will not be expensed. Rather, after a cost is capitalized, it will be systematically matched with the benefits it generates. In the case of the cost of inventory, the inventory will become cost of goods sold (an expense) when it is sold. In the case of plant and equipment, the capitalized cost will be depreciated over the useful life of the assets, thus matching its cost with its benefits. One exception is the cost of land. By definition, land is not a wasting asset and so it not depreciated.

b. Note A to the Consolidated Financial Statements provides very little information about the specific costs included in the "Land, primarily landfill sites" account. The note states that, "[l]andfill disposal sites, including land and related landfill preparation costs, are stated at cost." Based on this note, one would think that traditional purchase and "get ready" costs (e.g., clearing, bulldozing, surveys, etc.) are included in the balance.

c. The matching principle states that an entity should recognize as expenses the cost of producing goods or services in the same period those goods and services generate revenues. As you can see from this simple definition, the timing of revenue recognition determines the timing of expense recognition.

Conservatism is a more general concept in accounting. Basically, conservatism is a way for accountants to deal with uncertainty in a way that is meaningful to third-party users of financial information. That is, if doubt exists as to whether the earnings process is complete, a company likely should not recognize the related revenue. In addition, if doubt exists as to whether a cost is related to future revenue generating activities, it should be expensed in the period incurred. Therefore, conservatism is a guide that can be used in the application of the matching principle. If significant uncertainty exists with respect to the future benefit of a cost, then conservatism suggests that it should be expensed immediately.

d. i. These costs should have been immediately expensed. While the executives' efforts may have been directly related to future revenue generation, reliably matching their efforts to future revenues is difficult at best. Had Chambers kept detailed time records, there may have been a basis for capitalizing a portion of the salaries.

d. ii. Public relations expense is a classic period cost incurred by most large corporations. Matching this expense to future revenues also is difficult. Legal fees, on the other hand, occasionally are capitalized. A very common example is legal fees capitalized in connection with the successful defense of an entity's patent. In addition, legal fees directly related to acquiring a specific landfill site could also be capitalized without violating the spirit of matching or conservatism.

d. iii. SFAS No. 34 is very specific in allowing interest capitalization only in certain circumstances. In general, this standard only allows capitalization when an entity constructs long-lived assets. Interest expense associated with the *purchase* of revenue-producing assets usually is not allowed. Interest on debt specifically associated with the *development* of landfills could be capitalized. Note that although landfills (many of which are beyond the development stage and thus ineligible for interest capitalization) account for roughly half of Chambers' total assets, well over half (70%) of their 1990 interest was capitalized. This is an indication that Chambers' earnings may be of poor quality.

d. iv. This cost is similar to the cost incurred when a company temporarily rents production equipment when the main equipment in the factory is under repair. The future benefit is hard to measure and the revenues against which this expense should be recognized are the revenues collected from the specific waste being disposed of in the other companies' landfills.

d. v. While costs incurred in connection with the acquisition of other companies probably has some future benefit, it is difficult to identify the future periods from which the benefit will be realized. In addition, internal costs are difficult to verify. That is, it is difficult to identify what portion of an employee's efforts are directly related to future economic benefits.

e. The main tool at your disposal is to compare Chambers' annual reports to those of other companies in the waste-management business. A comprehensive comparison of Chambers' financial statements to those of other companies may have revealed excessive accruals and poor cash flow from operating activities. In addition, a number of financial services publish industry-wide statistics and ratios. Comparison to these ratios also may have revealed a situation that was too good to be true. The capitalization of interest (noted in part d. iii.) is an example. Another red flag is that revenue increased 42% in 1990 and landfill costs increased 71%! Over the same period, the same figures for Waste Management, Inc., a major competitor, were 37% and 30%. Although Chambers' numbers may be reflecting a high growth rate, they are nonetheless cause for further investigation.

f. The most obvious incentive derives from a compensation plan tied to operating income. In this case, management has an short-term incentive to understate expenses by capitalizing costs. In addition, management may own some of Chambers' common stock. While it is naive to believe that the stock market will misprice securities based on capitalization policy, there is plenty of anecdotal evidence in the financial press pointing to such beliefs. Whether such beliefs are rational is irrelevant as long as they are pervasive enough to affect management behavior.

Teaching Notes:

The distinction between U.S. GAAP and foreign GAAP is of increasing interest to users of financial statements. Currently, the SEC requires nearly all registrant companies to file financials prepared in accordance with U.S. GAAP regardless of jurisdiction of incorporation. The U.S. capital markets are becoming increasingly attractive to foreign corporations and critics of the conformance regulation claim that it needlessly deters market entry by otherwise desirable participants. Facility with foreign financials is a skill that will be of increasing importance.

Students find this case appealing because they are familiar with the company. We use this case early in the semester. Even though they do not have the accounting knowledge to evaluate these financials at a deep level by then, students can pick out the presentation differences.

The case also illustrates how different financial statement users can make different assumptions. Students will have different responses to the pro-forma part of the case. While there are some assumptions that are more "correct" than others, there is no "correct solution" to this case. The variety of solutions can lead to a discussion of the need to understand the particular assumptions and estimates that underlie a set of financial statements. This case points out nicely that accounting is more of an art than a science.

a. i.
- Assets are presented in the reverse order from that used by American companies: current assets are presented after fixed assets.
- Cash is presented last whereas in the U.S. it is the first asset listed.
- Current liabilities are not separately identified from long-term.
- Common stock and other equity accounts are called liabilities and come before what U.S. GAAP labels liabilities.

a. ii.
- There are three years' balance sheets versus two in the U.S.
- The gross balance of assets is presented in a column with a second column for depreciation or provision.

a. iii. The balance sheet is different in the following respects:
- Use of French Francs as unit of measurement (as opposed to U.S. dollars).
- Current assets include an account called equipment and real estate: these are considered fixed assets in the U.S.
- Foreign currency adjustment appears as an asset.
- Group net income is a liability account.
- There is a liability account labeled provisions and allowances: this could be a reserve for future losses which is not allowed under U.S. GAAP.
- Club Med's share of its subsidiaries' retained earnings is a separate line item rather than included in the total retained earnings.
- Net income for 1992 is not closed out to retained earnings.

Note: some of the differences between French and U.S. Balance Sheets are obvious from a cursory review of the Financial Statements. Others require more than a passing familiarity with the contents of Financial Statements. Still others require in-depth knowledge of GAAP. Don't be surprised if you didn't catch all these items.

a. iv. The solution involves assumptions about how current some assets and liabilities are. Answers will differ with different assumptions.

"Amounts received for future vacations" is probably unearned revenue (i.e., deposits) that will be earned within the next year. Most vacationers don't pay for trips more than a year in advance.

Analyzing the footnote "Bonds, banks, and other loans" we see that a portion of Long-term debts is currently due. The payments in 92/93 of 414,498 should be classified as current. Also, there is an amount called "Due to banks." Because this amount is distinguished from "long-term debt" in the footnote, it probably represents the drawn-down portion of the company's line of credit. This is a current liability.

CLUB MÉDITERRANÉE S.A.
CONSOLIDATED BALANCE SHEET
in thousands of FRF

ASSETS	October 31, 1992
Cash	665,930
Trade accounts receivable, net (allowance 29,103)	311,216
Other accounts receivable, net (allowance 5,587)	853,917
Inventories and work in progress, net (allowance for obsolescence 141)	169,305
Total current assets	2,000,368
Loans and advances	196,264
Debenture receivables and deposits	169,898
Investments in and advances to unconsolidated Subsidiaries and affiliates, net	471,269
Fixed assets	
Equipment and real estate	72,007
Property and equipment	8,632,878
Total fixed assets	8,704,885
less accumulated depreciation	(2,913,614)
Net fixed assets	5,791,271
Intangible assets, net (amortization 122,558)	901,718
Total assets	9,530,788
LIABILITIES	
Trade accounts payable	379,398
Other accounts payable	1,010,961
Amounts received for future vacations	312,322
Due to banks, see footnotes	349,318
Current portion of long-term debt, see footnotes	414,498
Total current liabilities	2,466,497
Bonds, banks and other loans, long-term portion	2,831,043
Minority interests	506,766
Shareholders' equity	
Common stock	272,120
Additional paid-in capital	1,385,247
Retained earnings of parent company (1,128,616 + net income 161,261 + RE of subs 640,737)	1,930,614
Provisions and allowances	177,264
Foreign currency translation adjustment (asset 58,260, liability 19,497)	(38,763)
Total shareholders' equity	2,154,362
Total liabilities and shareholders' equity	9,530,788

b. i.   The income statement is different in the following respects:

- French francs are used rather than U.S. dollars.
- Net income is not closed to retained earnings until after the balance sheet has been prepared.
- Goodwill amortization is deducted after income tax and extraordinary items.
- Extraordinary items (EI's) are not reported net of income taxes (they are reported before income taxes on the income statement). U.S. statements report EI's net of the related income taxes.
- Disposals of fixed assets are considered extraordinary items.
- Earnings per share calculations are not disclosed.

b. ii.   The accounting principles used by Club Med that would be informative include the basis for consolidation, the methods and rates used for depreciating fixed assets, the method and rate to depreciate intangibles, the basis for tax expense calculation, the foreign currency translation method and revenue recognition policies. This last item is the most important item because a small percentage change in revenue translates into a huge change in net income.

c.   Working capital is the difference between current assets and current liabilities. It is a measure of the cushion that Club Med has when it comes to paying off liabilities in the near term. Based on the balance sheet prepared in accordance with U.S. GAAP, Club Med has negative working capital of FRF 466,129 (2,000,368 - 2,466,497).

Current ratio is the ratio of current assets to current liabilities.

1992 Current ratio = 2,000,368 / 2,466,497 = 0.8110.

Quick ratio is "quick" assets divided by current liabilities. Quick assets are sometimes defined as Cash + Marketable Securities. The solution here uses Cash + Marketable Securities + Accounts Receivable. Either is OK. You should recognize that the main purpose of this ratio is to adjust the current ratio for relatively slow-moving current assets such as inventory. If you think A/R are slow moving, they should not be included in the numerator.

1992 Quick ratio = (665,930 + 853,917 + 311,216) / 2,466,497 = 0.7424.

At the end of fiscal 1992, short-term liquidity is not strong. Negative working capital and current and quick ratios less than 1.0 suggest that the company may have trouble paying its debts as they come due in the next year. The company is generating significant cash flows from operations which is a good sign. However, these have been decreasing over the last three years. Given these cash flows, the company seems to have the ability to repay some of its debt in the future and thus relieve some of the related interest costs (assuming the company stops reinvesting the cash flows in physical assets). These comments must be interpreted with caution because several assumptions were made in determining which items should be included as current.

Diageo plc—Adjusting Journal Entries

Teaching Notes:

The first portion of the case provides a contrast of foreign (U.K.) financial statements with U.S. GAAP statements. Part a can be used alone or as a lead-in to the accounting mechanics (transaction and adjusting journal entries) that follow. If the first part of the case is omitted, students would benefit from having the solution to that part as they complete the remainder of the case.

The second portion of the case requires students to consider adjusting journal entries in general (part b) and then to prepare journal entries (parts c through e). To create the transaction and adjusting journal entries, students must work backwards from the financial statements to the economic events that underlie the final numbers. If each adjusting journal entry is tied to the economic and business reasons that necessitate its preparation, students see the importance of the exercise. In class, students can be asked to speculate on the circumstances that gave rise to each adjustment. The discussion can be widened to include issues of internal control and risk. For example, the inventory ('stocks' in UK GAAP) adjustment is required to reconcile the books to the year-end inventory count. This leads to questions about how inventory is controlled during the year if there are no records and to the mechanics of an inventory count.

Recreating transaction journal entries (parts c and d) helps students link balance sheet and income statement accounts that are typically combined to capture transactions. For example, the debit side of a sales ('turnover' in UK GAAP) transaction is not immediately obvious to some students. Preparing a summary journal entry for sales (in part c) helps students to see the link. This lays the groundwork for later cases where students analyze the balance sheet effects of a revenue recognition issue.

In part e of the case, students are required to understand the mechanics of the adjustment process and will gain facility with journal entry preparation.

The process of financial statement preparation is new to many students (as is the world of business) and putting the adjusting journal entry exercise into a broader business context can make it rewarding.

The final portion of the case moves students away from the process and to analysis. It is important to stress early on that financial reports are prepared so that readers can assess an entity's financial position, its current and future profitability with a view to making decisions. Financial statements provide information only if users can 'use' them.

a. i.
- Use of pounds Sterling (£) as unit of measurement (as opposed to U.S.$).
- Two columns for each year, one column for subtotaled amounts, the other column for final totals.
- Liabilities shown in brackets.
- Assets are presented in the reverse order from that used by American companies: current assets are presented after fixed assets.
- Fixed assets include an account called investments. This is not considered a fixed asset under U.S. GAAP.
- No accumulated depreciation information (or even mention) for the fixed tangible assets.
- Cash is presented last in the current asset section whereas in the U.S. it is the first asset listed.
- Debtors due after a year are classified as current.
- A subtotal line shows net current liabilities or assets.
- There is a liability account labeled "provisions for liabilities and charges" this could be a reserve for future losses which is not allowed under U.S. GAAP.
- Revaluation reserve appears as an equity account. This is a write-up of long-term assets to market value. This is not permitted under U.S. GAAP.
- Minority interest is classified as a liability under U.S. GAAP, Diageo shows it after shareholders' equity.

U.K. GAAP terminology	U.G. GAAP equivalent
Intangible assets	same, or Patents, Trademarks, or Goodwill
Tangible assets	Property, plant, and equipment
Investments	Available for sale securities
	Securities held to maturity
	Investments at equity
Stocks	Inventory
Debtors due within one year	Trade and other receivables
Debtors due after one year	Long-term notes receivable
Investments	Marketable securities
Cash at bank and in hand	Cash and cash equivalents
Creditors due within one year	Current liabilities
Borrowings	Bank loans, notes payable
Other creditors	Accounts payable
Net current liabilities/assets	no equivalent
Creditors due after on year	Long-term debt
Borrowings	Bank loans, bonds payable
Other Creditors	Other long-term liabilities
Provision for liabs and charges	Other accrued liabilities (?)
Equity share capital	Common stock at par
Non-equity share capital	Preferred stock at par
Called-up share capital	Total stock at par
Share premium account	Capital in excess of par
Capital redemption reserve	no equivalent
Profit and loss account	Retained earnings (loss)
Reserves attributable	Total shareholder's equity
Minority interests - equity	same but classified in liabilities
Minority interests - nonequity	no equivalent

Note: some of the differences between U.K. and U.S. Balance Sheets are obvious from a cursory review of the Financial Statements. Others require more than a passing familiarity with the contents of Financial Statements. Still others require in-depth knowledge of GAAP. Don't be surprised if you didn't catch all these items.

a. ii.

Current assets	6,558
Fixed assets	9,720
Total assets	16,278
Current liabilities	7,437
Long-term liabilities	3,495
Provision for liabilities	753
Total liabilities	11,685
Called up share capital	992
Reserves attributable to	
equity shareholders	4,026
Minority interest	567
Total SH equity	4,593
Total liabilities and SH equity	16,278

a. iii.

- Use of pounds Sterling (£) as unit of measurement (as opposed to U.S.$).
- Separate columns for income before and after goodwill and exceptional items (EI's).
- EI's are not reported net of income taxes (they are reported before income taxes on the income statement). U.S. statements report EI's net of the related income taxes.
- Discontinued operations are more detailed than in U.S. and are set out in a separate section in the middle of the income statement.
- Utilisation of provision – shows reversal of prior accrual for discontinued operations. No equivalent in U.S. GAAP.

U.K. GAAP terminology	U.G. GAAP equivalent
Turnover	Revenue or Net sales
Change in stocks	Increase or decrease in inventory over the period. This is a part of Cost of Sales under U.S. GAAP.
Raw materials and consumables	Purchases of inventory. This too is part of Cost of Sales in the U.S.
Transferred to reserves	Net income added to retained earnings for the period

b. i. The Stocks account will require adjusting for the year-end inventory count, for goods in transit but not yet received, goods sold but not yet shipped, and for obsolete inventory. As well, goods may have been damaged or stolen and the accounts need to reflect this.

b. ii. Some of the "Debtors" (customers that have purchased goods on accounts receivable) may not pay. An Allowance for uncollectible accounts will need to be estimated and possibly adjusted. This contra-account is combined on Diageo's balance sheet with Debtors-due within one year. In addition, some credit sales may not yet have been included in turnover (sales revenue) if those sales had been earned but not yet billed. This will require an adjusting journal entry.

b. iii. Creditors due within one year (accounts and other payables) will require adjustment for charges and expenses that have been incurred by Diageo for which an invoice has not been received at year end. This account is also the account Diageo would probably use for interest, labor and other accruals required to match expenses to revenues (which is called turnover).

b. iv. Diageo records its day-to-day transactions, such as turnover (sales) and purchases, with transaction journal entries. Adjusting journal entries are typically made at the end of a financial reporting period. Balance sheet accounts that are likely candidates for adjustment include:

- Debtors due within one year might include items such as prepaid advertising. Diageo amortizes these costs beginning when the ad is first shown to the public. The expired portion of the prepayment would need to be expensed.
- Intangible fixed assets (such as patents, trademarks, goodwill) needs to be amortized in order to match its cost with the benefits it generates.

- Debtors subject to financing arrangements (franchisee loans) may have interest owing to Diageo and that will need to be accrued.
- Fixed tangible assets (property, plant, and equipment) will require an adjustment for depreciation for the year as well as for old equipment that is written off the books as worthless.
- Investments (both fixed and current) may be interest bearing (e.g. corporate or governmental bonds purchased as investments) and that interest revenue needs to be accrued if it has been earned but not received.
- Borrowings may be interest bearing (long-term liabilities, bank loans, and long-term debt surely are). An adjusting journal entry may need to made to record unpaid interest. Creditors due after one year (long-term debt) may need to be reclassified to 'Creditors due within one year' if a portion of it is due in the next year or operating cycle.
- Minority interests are typically not estimated until the end of the year when the tax liability is calculated.

c. i. From the profit and loss account (income statement): "Turnover – continuing operations" totals £11,795.

Dr.	Cash (A)	£875	
Dr.	Debtors—due within one year (A)	£10,920	
Cr.	Turnover – continuing operations (R)		£11,795

To record product sales made on account.

c. ii. From Note 4 to the profit and loss account (income statement): "Advertising, marketing and promotion expense" totals £1,647.

Dr.	Advertising, marketing and promotion expense or Operating costs (E)	£1,647	
Cr.	Cash (A)		£1,647

To record advertising expenses paid with cash and on account.

d. i. From the cash flow statement: "Purchase of tangible fixed assets" totals £534 (use).

Dr.	Purchase of tangible fixed assets (A)	£534	
Cr.	Cash at bank and in hand (A)		£534

To record cash purchases of fixed assets.

d. ii. From the cash flow statement: "Issue of share capital" totals £50 (source).

Dr.	Cash at bank and in hand (A)	£50.00	
Cr.	Equity share capital (OE)		£3.76*
Cr.	Share premium account (plug) (OE)		£46.24

To record proceeds received on sale of shares.

*13,000,000 shares x 28.935 *pence* par value per share (100 pence per pound)

e. i. From Note 4 to the profit and loss account (income statement): "Depreciation and other amounts written off fixed assets" totals £440.

Dr.	Depreciation and other amounts written off fixed assets, or Operating costs (E)	£440*	
Cr.	Fixed assets – Tangible and Intangible (A)		£440

To record depreciation on property and amortization on intangibles.

* Final balance less unadjusted trial balance: £440 – £0.

e. ii. From the case: "Interest payable", the liability, totals £435.

Dr.	Interest expense (called Interest payable (net) on the statement of profit and loss) (E)	£135*	
Cr.	Other creditors (L)		£135

To accrue interest owing to various creditors.

* Final balance less unadjusted trial balance: £435 – £300.

f. An important use of financial reports is to assist readers assess the nature and timing of the company's future cash flows and income. If some parts of the company's operations have been discontinued, cash flows and income from those segments cannot be counted on in the future. That is, they are not persistent cash flows or earnings. Knowing this helps financial statement users make more accurate predictions of continuing operations' cash flow and earnings. As well, certain expenses and losses might have been triggered when operations were discontinued. These losses are one-shot items, and again, because they are not persistent, they should not figure into a projection of future outcomes.

Teaching Notes:

In this case, students are required to first *find* information about Dow's common stock, then *explain* how repurchased shares are accounted for, and finally, *use* the treasury stock information to determine the cost of various ownership options.

We have found that a discussion of *why* companies buy back their own stock is very helpful. It provides an opportunity to integrate current news stories and research in finance and accounting. For example, we talk about Chrysler's announcement that it will buy back its stock in response to investor Kirk Kerkorian's plea to enhance shareholder value. We also discuss how stock repurchases can be used to signal management's belief that the shares are undervalued (we also discuss how it is important that such disclosures be credible—i.e., how do we know that a company whose managers do not believe their shares are undervalued is not trying to mimic a company whose managers truly do believe their shares are undervalued?)

These discussions take us out of the world of bookkeeping and into a broader business setting.

a. i.   According to the balance sheet, Dow is authorized to issue 500 million shares.

a. ii.   According to the balance sheet, Dow has issued 327,125,854 shares at December 31, 1999.

a. iii.   According to the balance sheet, 223,281,638 (issued: 327,125,854 shares less 103,844,216 in treasury) shares are outstanding at December 31, 1999.

a. iv.   There are numerous reasons why companies buy back their own shares. First, they may buy shares so that they can be reissued to employees under employee stock option plans. Doing so is much cheaper than issuing new shares. Second, they may do so to thwart a takeover attempt. Repurchasing shares leaves the outstanding shares in fewer, and potentially more-friendly, hands. Third, companies sometimes buy back their shares to signal that they think their shares are undervalued and, thus, a good value. Finally, when companies have excess cash and lack adequate investment opportunities they can repurchase their own shares. The companies' earnings thus accrue to a smaller pool of shares, in theory leading to enhanced shareholder value.

b. i.   According to Note L, 3.734 million shares were repurchased.

b. ii.   Total cost of the stock repurchased was $429 million. The average cost per share was $114.89 ($429 / 3.734 = $114.89).

b. iii.   In 1999, Dow issued 3.192 million shares to employees under option and purchase plans.

b. iv.   Note L states that Dow reissued 3,500,000 shares for $431 million (approximately $123.14 each) so it could use the pooling of interests method of accounting for its merger with Union Carbide.

c.   According to the balance sheet, Dow carries its treasury stock "at cost." Therefore, the company uses the *cost method*. Under this approach, the cost of treasury stock reacquired is shown as a "contra-equity account" in the shareholders' equity section of the balance sheet. The following journal entry summarizes Dow's treasury stock purchases for the year (in millions):

Dr.	Treasury stock, at cost	429
Cr.	Cash	429
	To record stock repurchase.	

An alternative method is called the *par value method*. Under this approach, the purchase of treasury shares is treated like a retirement of stock with the corresponding par and paid-in capital amounts subtracted from the accounts in the balance sheet. In general, the cost method more clearly portrays treasury stock as a tool available for business purposes like acquisitions and employee stock ownership plans.

d.   Assets are defined as expected future economic benefits. According to *SFAC* No. 6, shareholders' equity is the difference between assets and liabilities. It is basically the capital contributed to the company by its owners plus the income retained in the company (i.e., *not* paid out in dividends). Dow classifies its treasury stock as a contra equity account, even though it seems to use the shares as an asset. The reason treasury stock is not reported as an asset goes back to a very important component of the accounting model—that is, the entity concept in financial reporting.

e. i.

	Number of Shares
Shares "issued" at December 31, 1999	327,125,854
Less:	103,844,216
Shares "in treasury" at December 31, 1999	
Shares "outstanding" at December 31, 1999	223,281,638
	x 10%
10% of outstanding shares	22,328,164
Shares owned by BASF at December 31, 1999	13,396,898
Additional shares needed for BASF to have 10% interest in Dow	8,931,266

At an average price of $133.625, BASF will pay $1,193,440,419 for these shares. Dow does not book a journal entry for the stock sales and purchase activity of independent third parties.

e. ii.

	Number of Shares
Shares owned by BASF at December 31, 1999	13,396,898
	÷ 10%
Total shares outstanding required to give BASF a 10% interest	133,968,980
Shares outstanding at December 31, 1999	223,281,638
Shares to be purchased by Dow	89,312,658

At an average share price of $133.625, Dow would pay approximately $11.93 billion for these shares. The journal entry to record this hypothetical repurchase is (in millions):

```
Dr.   Treasury stock, at cost              11,930
Cr.        Cash                                        11,930
      To record stock repurchase.
```

Teaching notes:

Environmental concerns are a current hot topic in financial reporting. The SEC has, over the past few years, required increased disclosure of costs, expenses, accruals and future remediation plans. By comparison, the FASB has less stringent disclosure requirements which is obvious to students in this case, when they compare the MD&A (SEC's requirements) with the footnotes to the financials.

DuPont's total expense related to the environment was $800 million in 1996. Part of that was the remediation accrual. Another part was depreciation of previously capitalized environmental expenditures. The components of the total expense cannot all be estimated because insufficient evidence is provided.

The MD&A and the footnote are rather complicated. They contain lots of jargon and use accounting terms that may confuse some students. A common mistake is to confuse the $800 million (total expense) with the Superfund and RCRA remediations paid during the year.

The "contingency" surrounding Superfund and RCRA remediation is more complicated than most contingency estimation because of the "potentially responsible party" stance taken by the CERCLA. Corporations are not only responsible for their share of clean-up costs but responsible for the entire cost of a site clean-up. In order to book the accrual, DuPont must assess the likelihood of the other PRP's making good on their share of the costs. DuPont discusses the notion of total responsibility in their MD&A and assesses the financial stability of others named as PRP's. This is unique.

E.I. du Pont de Nemours—Environmental Matters

a. A contingent liability arises from an existing condition that may result in a negative outcome in the future. The unfavorable resolution of certain future event(s) may necessitate an economic sacrifice. Common examples of contingent liabilities include warranties, lawsuits, and uncollectibles.

b. Footnote 1 says "Accruals for environmental matters are recorded in operating expenses when it is <u>probable</u> that a liability has been incurred and the amount of the liability can be <u>reasonably estimated</u>." The underlined words are important concepts.

Under generally accepted accounting principles (GAAP), a contingency must be accrued at the financial statement date if two conditions are met:
    1) if it is highly probable (as opposed to remotely or reasonably probable) that a liability has been incurred. DuPont's note says "probable" which is less specific than GAAP. DuPont's approach could be construed as conservative.
    2) the amount of the loss can be reasonably estimated. DuPont discusses in the MD&A the ways it estimates its liability. It also makes disclaimers about the fact that the liability could be greater than estimated but that the company does not think that the worst case scenario is materially different than what they've disclosed.

c. The Management's Discussion and Analysis (MD&A) excerpt reveals that total environmental expense for the year amounted to, approximately, $800 million prior to adjusting for $100 million of insurance proceeds. Thus, about $700 million of environmental expense appears on the income statement (somewhere). From the details this appears to cover the following types of expenses:

Remediation accruals	91
less insurance proceeds	(100)
Solid waste management operations	180
Solid waste depreciation of capital	?
Research and development	?
Wastewater treatment facilities	180
Total pretax expense	700

The MD&A also mentions capital projects of $300. These amounts are related to the environment and have been set up as fixed assets. In future years these costs will be expensed as depreciation as was done in 1996 for previous years' capital outlays.

The expense amounts (totaling $700) would likely appear in "Cost of Goods Sold and Other Operating Charges." The depreciation and research components might have been included in those line items on the income statement.

d. As of December 31, 1996 DuPont had recorded a liability of $586 million. The liability had a balance of $602 million the year before.

These amounts are not shown as a separate line item on the balance sheet. In addition, the footnotes and the MD&A are silent on the exact location of the accruals. In all likelihood they are split into two accounts. The amounts that DuPont expects to expend in the coming year would be included in "Other accrued liabilities" in the current liabilities section. The amounts to be spent over the longer term (which DuPont says will be several decades!) would most likely be included in "Other Liabilities" with long-term liabilities.

e.
Dr.	Environmental expenses (COGS or other)		91
Cr.	Other Liabilities		91

To record remediation accrual (contingent liability account) for 1996.

f. i. The total drawdown of the contingent liability for Superfund remediation was, according to the MD&A, $28 million.

```
Dr.   Other Liabilities                               28
Cr.        Cash and/or accounts payable                       28
```
To record CERCLA costs paid during 1996.

f. ii. The total drawdown of the contingent liability for RCRA remediation was, according to the MD&A, $79 million.

```
Dr.   Other Liabilities                               79
Cr.        Cash and/or accounts payable                       79
```
To record RCRA costs paid during 1996.

g. i. DuPont has, at the end of 1996, numerous insurance claims outstanding. DuPont does not record insurance proceeds prior to receiving them. Potential gains on these claims are not recorded.

g. ii. It is not acceptable under U.S. GAAP for DuPont to accrue potential insurance gains because of their contingent nature. GAAP requires contingent gains not be recorded until realized (i.e., when they are no longer contingent on a future event occurring or failing to occur). GAAP further requires that contingent gains that are highly probable be disclosed in the footnotes. Note that under International Accounting Standards, expected insurance proceeds could be used to offset (i.e., net) the contingent liability (IAS 10, paragraph 8a).

This asymmetric treatment of environmental gains and losses is evidence of the conservative nature of accrual accounting.

g. iii. DuPont received $100 million from its insurers during 1996. The company recorded the receipt of cash and reduced current expenses. The costs related to the insurance proceeds may or may not have been actually paid by DuPont. The liability remains unchanged and when DuPont does pay the expenses it will reduce the accrual.

```
Dr. Cash                                             100
Cr.        Environmental expenses (COGS or other)            100
```
To record receipt of funds from insurance during 1996.

h. The accrual account(s) combined had the following activity during 1996:

Accrued environmental liability
(Other Liabilities Current and Long Term)

		602	Balance 12/31/95
		91	1996 Accrual
CERCLA costs paid in 1996	28		
RCRA costs paid in 1996	79		
		586	Balance 12/31/96

Refer to part c to see how the remediation accrual of $91 relates to the total environmental expense for the year. Note that the insurance proceeds of $100 do not affect the accrued liability. According to GAAP, contingent gains, such as insurance recoveries, are never accrued. Therefore, receipt of the cash is recorded as an offset to the environmental expense for the year.

i. The SEC is much more demanding than GAAP when it comes to environmental issues. Corporations reveal details in the MD&A that do not appear anywhere in the financial statements. The footnotes prepared by DuPont are in compliance with GAAP but the company would have received a comment letter from the SEC asking for more information had the MD&A contained so little information. The MD&A is of increasing importance and it is viewed as critical by the SEC. During 1994, for example, the SEC requested additional information from more than 700 corporate registrants who fully met GAAP but did not, in the SEC's opinion, provide sufficient detail about their activities in their MD&A.

Teaching notes:

Most students are intrigued by this lawsuit. The products are known to them and the financial reporting strategies taken by the adversaries are self evident.

This case works well if the events are considered chronologically. Part a. of the case builds the chronology for the rest of the questions. Students can be called on to elaborate upon the accounting implications and choices at each important date in the lawsuit's history.

The financial statement analysis portion of the case requires students to think in pro-forma mode.

a.

1976, Apr.	Suit started by Polaroid
1985, Oct. 11	Judgment against Kodak, Kodak appeals to Fed Circuit
1986, Jan. 9	Injunction: Kodak prohibited from further US sales
1986, Apr. 25	Federal Circuit denies Kodak's appeal
1986, Oct. 6	US Supreme Court denies Kodak's appeal
1989, May.-Nov.	Damages trial: Polaroid seeks $6.1 billion, Kodak offers $187 million
1990, Oct. 12	Damages judgment $909.5 million
1990, Oct. 26	Polaroid appeals amount Kodak files cross-appeal
1990, Dec. 31	Kodak records loss $888 million in I/S
1991, Jan. 25	Award amended $873.2 million
1991, Feb. 22	Polaroid appeals amount
1991, Mar. 8	Kodak files cross-appeal
1991, Mar. 19	Kodak pays into escrow $960.5 million
1991, July 15	Settlement: all actions dropped
1991, July	Polaroid receives $924.5 million
1991, Oct. 18	Employee files suit
1991, Dec. 31	Polaroid recognizes gain in I/S

b. In 1976, the contingency didn't meet the requirements for Kodak to accrue a liability. Under generally accepted accounting principles (GAAP), a contingency must be accrued at the financial statement date if it is highly probable (as opposed to remotely or reasonably probable) that a liability has been incurred and the amount of the loss can be reasonably estimated. In 1976 neither criterion could be met.

More importantly, Polaroid would likely have used the accrual information to argue their case. The accrual could have been construed by the courts as an admission of guilt on Kodak's part, a scenario Kodak certainly wanted to avoid. Additionally, Kodak wanted to avoid accruing this contingent liability because of its negative effect on financial ratios (profitability and solvency ratios).

c.

Dr.	Litigation judgment	888
Cr.	Payables	888

To record the judgment for Polaroid.

d. By December 31, 1991 Kodak had exhausted its appeals, both the Federal Circuit and the Supreme Court upheld the lower courts' decisions. The open appeal at the end of December 31, 1990 pertained to the amount of the damages and not to the case itself. It was clear at the end of 1990 that the liability was "highly probable." As well, the amount could be reasonably estimated. Thus both GAAP criteria for accrual of a contingent loss had been met and Kodak could not avoid taking the charge to income.

Subsequent to the fiscal year-end, but before the financial statements were issued, damages were amended to $873.2 million. Therefore the best estimate of the loss for the fiscal year-end financials, was the latest verdict from the court.

e. At the end of fiscal 1976 it would not have been acceptable under GAAP to accrue any gain because of its contingent nature. GAAP requires that contingent gains, such as damages from the lawsuit, not be recorded until realized (i.e., when they are no longer contingent on a future event occurring or failing to occur). GAAP further requires that contingent gains that are highly probable be disclosed in the footnotes. This is evidence of the conservative nature of accrual accounting.

f.

Dr.	Cash and Short-term investments	924.5
Cr.	Litigation settlement	871.6
Cr.	Employee incentives payable	50.0
Cr.	Payroll taxes payable	2.9

To record receipt of settlement from Kodak and to record allocation of litigation settlement payable to employees.

g. Because the award amount was on appeal at the end of 1990, the potential settlement represented a contingent gain to Polaroid. That is, not all the uncertainty surrounding the gain had been resolved. Polaroid's disclosures related to the lawsuit complied with GAAP and allowed readers of their financial statements to adjust them as they saw fit. This is another example of the importance of reading the notes to the statements.

h. The settlement, net of employee incentives, was $872 million. After income tax on the settlement, Polaroid was left with roughly $500 million. From the 1991 statement of cash flows we see that repayments of long-term debt was $159 million higher than it was for fiscal 1990. As well, preferred stock was repurchased which resulted in a cash outflow of $282 million. Lastly, cash at the end of the year was $80 million higher than the year before. Together these changes explain a use of cash of $521 million. In short, it appears that Polaroid reconfigured its capital structure by retiring debt and preferred stock.

i. The earnings of Kodak and Polaroid reflect a "one-time" charge and gain respectively. In order to capitalize earnings and value each company, you would want to back these items out of reported earnings. It is important to use only those earnings you consider permanent, or persistent (as opposed to transitory) in determining the value of a company under this method.

Teaching Notes:

In this case, students learn about a very current issue – the immediate write-off of acquired in-process research and development costs (IPR&D). The case highlights the mixed research and development (R&D) accounting treatments that prevail under current GAAP. These disparities can form the basis for in-class discussion of the political process of standard setting.

SFAS No. 2 "Accounting for Research and Development Costs" requires that all R&D costs be expensed in the period incurred. The FASB believed that the degree of uncertainty with respect to future benefits causes R&D costs to fail the measurability test.

There is one exception to SFAS No. 2. SFAS No. 86, "Accounting for the Cost of Computer Software to be Sold, Leased, or Otherwise Marketed" permits the capitalization of some software development costs (but not research costs) if certain criteria are met. The historical conditions (strong Silicon Valley lobbying efforts) that led to this "capitalize and amortize" treatment can be reviewed in conjunction with the eBay case. Other types of development expenditures (for example, drug related) are to be immediately expensed (per SFAS No. 2).

Purchased research and development costs are treated in a manner consistent with SFAS No. 2 – unless the acquired R&D costs meet the test of alternative future use, the costs are to be expensed at the consummation of the merger or acquisition (see FASB Interpretation 4). Corporate acquirers generally prefer immediately expensing IPR&D against earnings rather than capitalizing and amortizing such expenditures over time. Firms have been taking increasingly aggressive write-offs (e.g. IBM purchase of Lotus in 1995, Texas Instruments purchase of Amati in 1997). In 1999, the SEC sent more than 100 comment letters to companies requesting additional information about IPR&D write-offs in connection with acquisitions. Many revised their estimates downward in subsequent quarters. The topic is contentious and the FASB has added this item to its larger R&D project.

We have found that students easily understand the basic idea of capitalizing R&D costs that are expected to have future benefits. However, some students have trouble with the analysis part of the case (part h.) In particular, they struggle with the concept of adding back in-process R&D costs written off perhaps because it involves thinking backwards. Having them come up with journal entries often helps these students see the issue more clearly.

a. In general, In-Process Research and Development (IPR&D) are research and development projects acquired in a corporate merger or acquisition. IPR&D costs might include:

- wages, benefits, pensions, and other employment related expenses for R & D personnel
- supplies necessary to conduct research
- research facilities and equipment which would be capitalized as fixed assets and charged to R & D as depreciation
- legal costs associated with patent applications
- overhead charges for personnel related indirectly to R & D
- research related travel, conference fees, costs to host conferences
- cost of academic publications subscribed to by R & D personnel

b. eBay expensed $150,000 of IPR&D immediately upon acquiring Jump Inc.

c. eBay determined that, of the total intangible assets acquired from Jump Inc., $150,000 represented the fair-value of research begun but not completed by Jump for which eBay had no future commercial use.

d. In a merger or acquisition, the buyer assigns the total purchase price among all identifiable tangible and intangible assets. Research and Development costs are one type of identifiable intangible assets. If acquired IPR&D costs meet the 'future alternative use' criterion set out in Financial Accounting Standards Board Statement No. 2, "Accounting for Research and Development" then the IPR&D may be capitalized and amortized. Otherwise, if the IPR&D does not meet the SFAS 2 criterion, then the costs must be expensed at the consummation of the acquisition.

This treatment does not acknowledge the fair value of all assets acquired and opens the door to potential abuse. Firms may prefer to take a large one-time write-off after an acquisition in order to manage future earnings growth. Firms have, over the past several years, exercised considerable latitude in how they assign costs to IPR&D and large write-offs have increasingly come under SEC scrutiny.

In the case of eBay, Jump Inc. was a basket of inseparable intellectual assets. Allocating $150,000 to in-process technology was arbitrary. Jump's worth will likely be valuable to eBay for more than a year. The fact that eBay was willing to pay $150,000 for the IPR&D is evidence of the value of the asset.

e. An alternative accounting treatment would be to identify potential future benefits arising from IPR&D and capitalize and amortize costs for which there are identified benefits. This is the approach taken by a number of countries (Canada, the Netherlands, Japan, etc.). This treatment can provide a better matching of costs and benefits because deferred development costs will be amortized when commercial production starts (and revenues are being earned). However, an associated drawback is that there is some uncertainty related to recoverability of IPR&D costs.

f.

Dr.	In-process R&D costs (expense)	150,000
Dr.	Purchased technology	500,000
Dr.	Covenants not to compete	208,000
Dr.	Customer list	1,484,000
Dr.	Goodwill	24,000
Cr.	Current liabilities	31,000
Cr.	Cash (plug)	335,000
Cr.	Common stock	2,000,000

To record acquisition of Jump Inc.

g. During the year, the amortization on the acquired Jump Inc. intangibles amounted to $1,030,000 (see footnote 3). In addition, the immediate write-off of the IPR&D was $150,000. In total, the income statement impact of the acquisition was $1,180,000 in 1998. In 1999, the balance of the acquired intangible assets will be expensed – eBay's policy is to amortize such costs over 8 to 24 months and it appears from footnote 3, that about half was amortized in 1998 leaving the remainder to be amortized in 1999.

h. Had eBay capitalized the IPR&D costs of $150,000 and amortized these costs in the same proportion as the costs they did capitalize, amortization expense would have increased by $150,000 * 1,030 / 2,216 = $70,000. Before tax, net income would have increased by $150,000 – $70,000 = $80,000. The after-tax effect, assuming a tax rate of 35%, would have been an increase in net income of $52,000. Considering that reported net income was $2,398,000 this would not have been a material difference.

i. It appears from Note 2, that eBay estimated the fair-value of the other intangible assets acquired first and that IPR&D of $150,000 was the plug. In any event, assigning a value to IPR&D is rather arbitrary.

j. Managers can manage earnings and other financial performance measures by strategically determining the amount to allocate to IPR&D. For example, management could choose to allocate a small proportion of the overall purchase price paid as IPR&D and thereby minimize the impact on the current period income statement. When net income is near an important threshold (say in a debt covenant, or zero net income, or last year's earnings) management might understate IPR&D costs and take as small a write-off as possible.

On the other hand, management might maximize the IPR&D write-off in a particularly good year (smoothing earnings) or in a particularly poor year (take a "big bath"). Financial analysts focus on earnings growth, and in the year after a large write-down, earnings will be much higher by comparison.

Many high tech ".com" companies have adopted the strategy of writing off as much of their IPR&D as possible. They are already in loss positions and adding to them won't make things any worse. Many analysts focus on top line (revenue) growth at .com companies in lieu of earnings (although that trend may be short lived as the firms run out of cash and investor patience).

eBay, however, is known as the exception to the .com rule in that they are profitable. As such, their incentive may be to minimize IPR&D to remain "in the black."

Food Lion, Inc.—Preparation of Financial Statements

Teaching Notes:

This case introduces students to the preparation of financial statements. Students are required, first, to consider the industry in which Food Lion operates and determine the kinds of line items that would appear on the company's balance sheet. Thus, the case forces students to consider the environment in which the company operates.

The case is designed to teach students to use a computer spreadsheet. The case provides guidance on how the spreadsheet should be set up so that students get immediate feedback about their progress. The case includes a suggested spreadsheet lay-out and recommends that income statement transactions NOT be posted directly to retained earnings. The spreadsheet has subtotals for the unadjusted and pre and post-closing trial balances. Facility with computer spreadsheets is a must for business professionals. Acquiring those skills takes time and practice. Thus, students ought to be discouraged, in our opinion from photocopying the casebook spreadsheet and writing in the journal entries by hand in lieu of using a computerized spreadsheet

Students are required to record journal entries for a series of transactions and adjustments. Two of the more complicated journal entries have been provided for the students. Students use the information from the spreadsheet to prepare a balance sheet and an income statement.

A classroom approach to this case is to have students handle each transaction and adjusting entry in turn. If classroom facilities permit, a computerized spreadsheet could be projected onto a screen and the instructor could fill in the cells, posting the journal entries as the class proceeds. Manually posting the entries to an overhead slide of the spreadsheet would serve the same purpose. The idea is that parts b and c can be done concurrently as can parts f and g.

As each journal entry is posted to cash, ask students whether the cash flow is an operating, investing, or financing cash flow. That will take care of part k of the case simultaneously.

We have included the actual December 28, 1996 Food Lion balance sheets and income statements at the end of this solution.

a.   Grocery store chains are just like any other retail chain. They acquire inventory from various sources, mark it up, and sell it. Thus, we would expect inventory to be a major asset. Another major asset would be the actual grocery stores (if owned or rented under capital lease). We wouldn't expect much in the way of accounts receivable because the grocery business is essentially cash-based. The liability side of the balance sheet likely includes major balances for accounts payable (mainly financing the inventory) and long-term debt associated with the properties.

b.

1.	Dr.	Inventories	7,222,670	
	Cr.	Current Liabilities		7,222,670
		To record purchase of inventory		
2.	Dr.	Cash	8,476,918	
	Cr.	Net Sales		8,476,918
		To record cash sales		
	Dr.	Cost of Goods Gold	6,661,516	
	Cr.	Inventories		6,661,516
		To record cost of inventory sold for cash		
3.	Dr.	Receivables	529,014	
	Cr.	Net Sales		529,014
		To record credit sales		
	Dr.	Cost of Goods Sold	410,409	
	Cr.	Inventories		410,409
		To record cost of inventory sold on account		
4.	Dr.	Current Liabilities	7,115,247	
	Cr.	Cash		7,115,247
		To record payment of accounts payable to suppliers		
5.	Dr.	Selling and Administrative Expenses	1,252,553	
	Cr.	Cash		1,252,553
		To record payment of wages and other expenses		
6.	Dr.	Cash	250,010	
	Cr.	Current Liabilities		250,010
		To record issuance of short-term note		
7.	No entry because a transaction has not occurred.			
8.	Dr.	Cash	505,846	
	Cr.	Receivables		505,846
		To record collection of receivables		
9.	Dr.	Property, at cost less Depreciation	283,564	
	Cr.	Cash		283,564
		To record acquisition of property		

```
10.  Dr.    Noncurrent Liabilities                         83,420
     Cr.         Cash                                                  83,420
            To record repayment of long-term debt

11.  Dr.    Inventories                                    49,229
     Dr.    Property, at cost less Depreciation            103,078
     Dr.    Goodwill                                       269,348
     Cr.         Cash                                                 121,578
     Cr.         Noncurrent Liabilities                               300,077
            To record acquisition of Kash 'n Karry chain of stores

12.  Dr.    Cash                                           27,464
     Dr.    Selling and Administrative Expenses               466
     Cr.         Property, at cost less Depreciation                   27,930
            To record disposal of fixed assets at a loss

13.  Dr.    Interest Expense                               76,631
     Cr.         Cash                                                  76,631
            To record payment of interest
```

14. No entry. Any increase in wages will be on the income statement for the following fiscal year when the wages are earned.

```
15.  Dr.    Noncurrent Liabilities                         12,258
     Cr.         Cash                                                  12,258
            To record payment of noncurrent liabilities

16.  Dr.    Cash                                            3,086
     Cr.         Contributed Capital (common stock)                     3,086
            To record issuance of stock

17.  Dr.    Property, at cost less Depreciation            97,595
     Dr.    Goodwill & Noncurrent Assets                   12,703
     Dr.    Contributed Capital                             4,412
     Dr.    Retained Earnings                              39,006
     Cr.         Current Liabilities                                   31,500
     Cr.         Noncurrent Liabilities                                77,871
     Cr.         Cash                                                  44,345
            To record lease, debt and stock repurchase transactions

18.  Dr.    Retained Earnings                              52,310
     Cr.         Cash                                                  52,310
            To record declaration and payment of dividends

19.  Dr.    Income Tax Provision                          131,700
     Dr.    Prepaid Expenses & Other                       25,789
     Dr.    Goodwill & Noncurrent Assets                    3,511
     Cr.         Cash                                                 155,422
     Cr.         Current Liabilities                                    5,578
            To record prepayment of income taxes for the year

20.  Dr.    Prepaid Expenses                               33,660
     Cr.         Cash                                                  33,660
            To record prepayment of insurance
```

c.   The spreadsheet follows at the end of the solution.

d. Unadjusted trial balance:

Account	Dr.	Cr.
Cash and Cash Equivalents	102,371	
Receivables	151,163	
Inventories	1,080,995	
Prepaid Expenses and Other	132,811	
Property, at Cost, less Depreciation	1,947,376	
Intangibles and Other Assets	287,345	
Current Liabilities		1,093,206
Noncurrent Liabilities		1,126,330
Contributed Capital		236,242
Retained Earnings		773,626
Net Sales		9,005,932
Cost of Goods Sold	7,071,925	
Selling and Administrative Expenses	1,253,019	
Depreciation and Depreciation	0	
Asset Impairment	0	
Interest Expense	76,631	
Income Tax Provision	131,700	
Total	12,235,336	12,235,336

e.
1. Accounts receivable need to be adjusted for uncollectible accounts.
2. Inventory has not yet been adjusted for the final inventory count. Stolen, obsolete and spoiled inventory needs to be written off.
3. Prepaid expenses needs to be adjusted for expired costs.
4. Depreciation needs to be recorded on the PPE.
5. Current liabilities need to be adjusted for accrued costs such as wages payable and interest payable. In addition, there may be amounts presently classified as noncurrent that will come due in the next year. These need to be reclassified as current.

f.

21.	Dr.	Cost of Goods Sold	15,252	
	Cr.	Inventories		15,252
		To adjust ending inventory to physical count		

22.	Dr.	Selling and Administrative Expense (Wages)	49,229	
	Cr.	Current Liabilities		49,229
		To record wages payable		

23.	Dr.	Selling and Administrative Expense (Insurance)	23,344	
	Cr.	Prepaid Expenses		23,344
		To adjust prepaid expense account		

24.	Dr.	Depreciation and Amortization Expense	165,286	
	Cr.	Property, at cost less Depreciation		165,286
		To record depreciation expense		

25.	Dr.	Noncurrent Liabilities	7,911	
	Cr.	Current Liabilities		7,911
		To reclassify current and long-term debt		

26.	Dr.	Interest Expense	3,889	
	Cr.	Current Liabilities		3,889
		To accrue interest expense		

27.	Dr.	Asset Impairment	9,587	
	Cr.	Property, at cost less Depreciation		9,587
		To record permanent impairment to assets		

g. The spreadsheet follows at the end of the solution.

h. Income statement for the year ended December 28, 1996:

Sales	9,005,932
Cost of Goods Sold	7,087,177
Selling and Administrative Expenses	1,325,592
Depreciation and Amortization	165,286
Asset Impairment	9,587
Interest Expense	80,520
Income Tax Provision	131,700
Net Income	206,070

i. The following journal entry closes the temporary accounts (the accounts on the income statement). Closing accounts with credit balances (Net Sales, for e.g.) requires a debit. Closing accounts with debit balances (all the expense accounts) requires credits. The difference (i.e. Net Income) is credited to Retained earnings.

Dr.	Sales	9,005,932	
Cr.	Cost of Goods Sold		7,087,177
Cr.	Selling and Administrative Expenses		1,325,592
Cr.	Depreciation and Amortization		165,286
Cr.	Asset Impairment		9,587
Cr.	Interest Expense		80,520
Cr.	Income Tax Expense		131,700
Cr.	Retained Earnings		206,070

To close temporary accounts to retained earnings.

j. December 28, 1996 balance sheet.

Current Assets

Cash and Cash Equivalents	102,371
Receivables	151,163
Inventories	1,065,743
Prepaid Expenses and Other Current Assets	109,467
Total current assets	1,428,744
Property, at cost less Depreciation	1,772,503
Goodwill and Noncurrent Assets	287,345
Total assets	3,488,592
Current Liabilities	1,154,235
Noncurrent Liabilities	1,118,419
Contributed Capital	236,242
Retained Earnings	979,696
Total liabilities and equity	3,488,592

k.

Transaction description	Type of transaction
1. Purchase groceries	Operating
2. Cash sales	Operating
3. Credit sales	Operating (but not an actual cash flow, see 8)
4. Pay accounts payable	Operating
5. Wages and other expenses	Operating
6. Note Payable	Financing
8. Collect receivables	Operating
9. Acquire PP&E	Investing
10. Repay LT debt	Financing
11. Kash n Karry	Investing
12. Disposal of PPE	Operating and Investing
13. Interest payments	Operating
15. Pay noncurrent liabs.	Operating
16. Issue Class A shares	Financing
17. Leases, debt and stock	Financing (per case, only stock transaction was for cash)
18. Pay dividends	Financing
19. Income tax expense	Operating (cash portion)
20. Insurance policy	Operating
21. Inventory count	Operating (but not an actual cash flow, see 1)
22. Accrue wages	Operating (but not an actual cash flow, see 5)
23. Adjust prepaid expenses	Operating (but not an actual cash flow, see 20)
24. Depreciation	Operating (but not an actual cash flow, see 9)
25. Reclassify LT debt	Financing (but not an actual cash flow)
26. Accrue interest	Operating (but not an actual cash flow, see 13)
27. Record asset impairment	Operating (but not an actual cash flow, see 9)

Food Lion, Inc. Asset accounts (in $000's)	Cash & Cash Equivalents		Receivables		Inventories		Prepaid Expenses & Other Current Assets		Property, at Cost, Less Depreciation		Goodwill & Noncurrent Assets	
	Debit (+)	Credit (-)	Debit (+)	Credit (-)	Debit (+)	Credit (-)	Debit (+)	Credit (-)	Debit (+)	Credit (-)	Debit (+)	Credit (-)
Balance Dec. 30, 1995	70,035		127,995		881,021		73,362		1,491,069		1,783	
Transactions:												
1. Purchase inventories					7,222,670							
2. Cash sales	8,176,918					6,661,516						
3. Credit sales			529,014			410,409						
4. Pay accounts payable		7,115,247										
5. Pay wages		1,252,553										
6. Issue short-term note	250,010											
7. no entry												
8. Collect receivables	505,846			505,846								
9. Acquire property		283,564							283,564			
10. Pay long-term debt		83,420										
11. Kash 'n Karry		121,578			49,229				103,078		269,348	
12. Dispose of property	27,464									27,930		
13. Pay interest		76,631										
14. no entry												
15. Pay liabilities		12,258										
16. Issue stock	3,086											
17. Leases, debt, & stock		44,345							97,595		12,703	
18. Pay dividends		52,310										
19. Income tax expense		155,422					25,789					
20. Prepay insurance		33,660					33,660					
Unadjusted trial balance	802,371		151,163		1,080,995		132,811		1,947,376		287,345	
Adjustments:												
21. Inventory count						15,252						
22. Accrue wages												
23. Amortize prepaids								23,344				
24. Depreciate property										165,286		
25. Reclassify debt												
26. Accrue interest												
27. Property impairment										9,587		
Pre-closing balances	802,371		151,163		1,065,743		109,467		1,772,503		287,345	
i) Closing entry												
Post-closing balances	802,371		151,163		1,065,743		109,467		1,772,503		287,345	
December 28, 1996 Actual Balance Sheet	802,371		151,163		1,065,743		109,467		1,772,503		287,345	

Food Lion, Inc.
Liability and SH equity

	Current Liabilities		Noncurrent Liabilities		Contributed Capital		Retained Earnings	
	Debit (-)	Credit (+)	Debit (-)	Credit (+)	Debit (-)	Credit (+)	Debit (-)	Credit (+)
Balance Dec. 30, 1995		698,695		844,060		237,568		864,942
Transactions:								
1. Purchase inventories		7,222,670						
2. Cash sales								
3. Credit sales								
4. Pay accounts payable	7,115,247							
5. Pay wages								
6. Issue short-term note		250,010						
7. no entry								
8. Collect receivables								
9. Acquire property			83,420					
10. Pay long-term debt								
11. Kash 'n Karry				300,077				
12. Dispose of property								
13. Pay interest								
14. no entry								
15. Pay liabilities			12,258					
16. Issue stock						3,086		
17. Leases, debt, & stock		31,500		77,871	4,412		39,006	
18. Pay dividends							52,310	
19. Income tax expense		5,578						
20. Prepay insurance								
Unadjusted trial balance		1,093,206		1,126,330		236,242		773,626
Adjustments:								
21. Inventory count								
22. Accrue wages		49,229						
23. Amortize prepaids								
24. Depreciate property								
25. Reclassify debt		7,911	7,911					
26. Accrue interest		3,889						
27 Property impairment								
Pre-closing balances		1,154,235		1,118,419		236,242		773,626
i) Closing entry								206,070
Post-closing balances		1,154,235		1,118,419		236,242		979,696
December 28, 1996 Actual Balance Sheet		1,154,235		1,118,419		236,242		979,696

Food Lion, Inc.
Income Stmt accounts

	Net Sales		Cost of Goods Sold		S&A Expenses		Depreciation and Amortization		Asset Impairment		Interest expense		Income Tax Provision (expense)		Total Debits	Total Credits
	Debit (-)	Credit (+)	Debit (+)	Credit (-)	Debit (+)	Credit (-)	Debit (+)	Credit (-)	Debit (+)	Credit (-)	Debit (+)	Credit (-)	Debit (+)	Debit (+)		
Balances Dec. 30, 1995		0	0		0		0		0		0		0		2,645,265	2,645,265
Transactions:																
1. Purchase inventories															7,222,670	7,222,670
2. Cash sales		8,476,918	6,661,516												15,138,434	15,138,434
3. Credit sales		529,014	410,409												939,423	939,423
4. Pay accounts payable															7,115,247	7,115,247
5. Pay wages					1,252,553										1,252,553	1,252,553
6. Issue short-term note															250,010	250,010
7. no entry																
8. Collect receivables															505,846	505,846
9. Acquire property															283,564	283,564
10. Pay long-term debt															83,420	83,420
11. Kash 'n Karry															421,655	421,655
12. Dispose of property					466										27,930	27,930
13. Pay interest											76,631				76,631	76,631
14. no entry															0	0
15. Pay liabilities															12,258	12,258
16. Issue stock															3,086	3,086
17. Leases, debt, & stock															153,716	153,716
18. Pay dividends															52,310	52,310
19. Income tax expense													131,700		161,000	161,000
20. Prepay insurance															33,660	33,660
Unadjusted trial balance		9,005,932	7,071,925		1,253,019		0		0		76,531		131,700		12,235,336	12,235,336
Adjustments:																
21. Inventory count			15,252												15,252	15,252
22. Accrue wages					49,229										49,229	49,229
23. Amortize prepaids					23,344										23,344	23,344
24. Depreciate property							155,236								165,286	165,286
25. Reclassify debt															7,911	7,911
26. Accrue interest											3,889				3,889	3,889
27 Property impairment									9,587						9,587	9,587
Pre-closing balances	9,005,932		7,087,177		1,325,592		155,236		9,587		80,520		131,700		12,288,454	12,288,454
i) Closing entry	9,005,932			7,087,177		1,325,592		165,286		9,587		80,520	131,700		9,005,932	9,005,932
Post-closing balances	0		0		0		0		0		0		0			
December 28, 1996																
Actual Income Statement		9,005,932	7,087,177		1,325,592		165,286		9,587		80,520		131,700		3,488,592	3,488,592

Frederick's of Hollywood—Property, Plant, & Equipment

Teaching notes:

Students are asked to recreate the activity in the property and equipment accounts. The gross PP&E and the accumulated depreciation account are analyzed using T-accounts. Frederick's operations are sufficiently straightforward to permit this exercise. While brighter students might find this exercise easy, it serves to reinforce the relationships among the income statement and balance sheet accounts related to PP&E.

Journal entries are used here to reinforce the connection between non-cash transactions (such as the disposal of PP&E in this question) and the related income statement effect. The case emphasizes that gains and losses do not affect cash, they are calculated numbers and depend on the depreciation method used.

The choice of accounting policy matters for a number of reasons. Capital markets pay attention to a company's bottom line. The discussion part of the case brings these facts to light. Students begin to see the strategic importance of accounting numbers.

a. The company could own its warehouse or some of the buildings where stores are located. Fixed assets would therefore include land and buildings. At each retail location, Frederick's fixed assets would include store shelving, racks, cash registers, and mannequins. Because the preponderance of its operations are likely in malls where space is leased and not owned, permanent changes made to the premises would be capitalized as leasehold improvements. This would include carpeting, painting, lighting, window displays and changing rooms that were constructed. Frederick's likely owns computers, telephones, desks, file cabinets and other furniture at the corporate offices and at the mail-order locations. There could also be company vehicles included as fixed assets.

b. The balance sheet includes "Property under capital leases" which indicates that Frederick's leases some of its fixed assets. Note six discloses that these assets are office equipment. This could be computers, printers, photocopiers, fax machines, and telephone equipment among others. This leased equipment is included with the assets that Frederick's owns outright because the company has all the rights and obligations of ownership over the leased assets. These leases, called capital leases are not to be confused with the operating leases for mall space that the company enters into.

c. This is probably the easiest question in accounting. Here's the rule to live by: Never depreciate land. (Of course, this is not to be confused with depletion accounting for natural resources—e.g., mining companies.)

d. Footnote one describes Frederick's depreciation policy. Buildings are depreciated over 10 to 25 years and other equipment from 4 to 10 years. The leasehold improvements are amortized over the shorter of the leased asset's useful life or the term of the lease. These policies seem appropriate given the nature of the assets and the firm's operations.

In choosing a depreciation policy, management is choosing how to allocate the cost of the asset to its useful life. This entails an estimate of the useful life of the asset and a decision of how best to *match* the initial cost to the periods the asset will be used. This choice is important for a number of reasons.

First, the accounting policy can have a significant effect on the net income of the company. As you will see in part g, depreciation patterns are very different across commonly used depreciation methods. This is especially true when the firm operates in a capital intensive industry, such as manufacturing. The policy can have a significant impact on key financial ratios such as earnings per share, return on assets, and other numbers that are used by shareholders in evaluating the company.

Second, the company may want to choose a policy that conforms to the one commonly used in their industry. Analysts and investors typically make comparisons across companies in the same industry and using the same policy facilitates those comparisons.

Third, the company may have debt covenants affected by the depreciation method choice. For example, a credit agreement may require the company to maintain a certain balance in retained earnings. Depreciation expense may determine whether the company violates this type of restriction.

Last, managerial compensation can also be affected by the choice of depreciation policy if compensation contracts are based on accounting numbers.

e. The activity in the gross equipment account and in the accumulated depreciation account can be analyzed using T-accounts, as follows.

(000's omitted)

Property and Equipment

Beg. Bal.	34,863		
Additions		Disposals	
(SCF)	4,073	1,424 (plug)	
End. Bal.	37,512		

Accumulated Depreciation

		16,638	Beg. Bal.
Disposals			Expense
(plug)	1,333	4,174	(SCF)
		19,479	End. Bal.

f. Using the information from the T-accounts above we can calculate the non-cash book loss on the disposal as follows:

Original cost of disposals	$ 1,424,000
Related accumulated depreciation	1,333,000
Net book value of disposals	91,000
Proceeds from the SCF	7,000
Book loss (non-cash) on disposal	$84,000

Dr.	Cash	7,000
Dr.	Accumulated Depreciation	1,333,000
Dr.	Loss on sale of fixed assets	84,000
Cr.	Property and Equipment	1,424,000

To record the sale of property and equipment at less than book value.

g.

Method	Base	Year 1	Year 2	Year 3	Year 4	Year 5
Depreciation expense						
SL (20%)	3,500	700	700	700	700	700
DDB (40%)	4,073	1,629	978	586	307	0*
Accumulated Depreciation						
SL		700	1,400	2,100	2,800	3,500
DDB		1,629	2,607	3,193	3,500	3,500
Net Book Value (Cost − Accumulated Depreciation)						
SL		3,373.	2,673	1,973	1,273	573
DDB		2,444	1,466	880	573	573

*By the end of year 5, we need to bring the net book value of the equipment down to the salvage value of $573. Therefore, we take the remaining depreciation in year 5. Alternatively, some companies switch from DDB to SL when SL depreciation would be greater than DDB. Ultimately, this achieves the same result: allocating the original cost of the equipment to the periods that it provides benefits.

h. i. Straight line

Original cost of disposals	$ 4,073,000	
Related accumulated depreciation	700,000	(1 year)
Net book value of disposals	3,373,000	
Proceeds	3,200,000	
Book loss (non-cash) on disposal	173,000	

Dr.	Cash	3,200,000	
Dr.	Accumulated Depreciation	700,000	
Dr.	Loss on sale of fixed assets	173,000	
Cr.	Property and Equipment		4,073,000

To record the sale of property and equipment for less than book value.

h. ii. Double-declining balance

Original cost of disposals	$ 4,073,000	
Related accumulated depreciation	1,629,000	(1 year)
Net book value of disposals	2,444,000	
Proceeds	3,200,000	
Book gain (non-cash) on disposal	756,000	

Dr.	Cash	3,200,000	
Dr.	Accumulated Depreciation	1,629,000	
Cr.	Property and Equipment		4,073,000
Cr.	Gain on sale of fixed assets		756,000

To record the sale of property and equipment for more than book value.

i. Fixed-asset turnover ratio

	Fiscal 1996	Fiscal 1995
Sales	$148,090	$142,931
Average net PP&E	($18,225 + $18,033)/2	($19,892 + $18,225)/2
	= $18,129	= $19,059
Turnover ratio	8.17	7.50

Frederick's fixed asset turnover ratio has increased during 1996. This is attributable to two factors. First, sales have increased 4% during 1996 from $142,931 to $148,090. Second, the fixed assets are older and have a net book value in 1996 less than that in 1995. The increased numerator and the decreased denominator jointly contribute to the higher turnover ratio in 1996. Overall, the change in the ratio is positive news. Frederick's is generating more sales per dollar invested in fixed assets in 1996.

Teaching Notes:

The Statement of Cash Flows (SCF) is a gold mine of information about a company's operating, financing, and investing activities. The Frederick's of Hollywood case serves to both introduce to students the statement and its uses, and to highlight the mechanics behind statement presentation, by having students recreate a portion of the SCF.

The early parts of the case highlight the differences between the SCF and the income statement (NOTE: Frederick's uses the term "Statement of Operations" to describe its income statement) and introduce the three sections of the SCF. The differences among the three parts of the SCF can be reinforced by relating each balance sheet account to one or more of the parts. If students understand what assets and liabilities relate to operations, investing and financing, preparation of the SCF becomes easier.

In the "Process" section of the case, students are asked to recreate the Statement of Cash Flows using balance sheet, income statement and footnote information only. Frederick's operations are sufficiently straightforward to permit this exercise. Challenges include using footnotes to determine fixed asset additions and depreciation charges and inferring deferred charges from changes in their related balance sheet liability accounts. The case breaks down these transactions to simplify the task. Analysis of the deferred tax accounts will be difficult if the case is used early in the semester, but because the final SCF is included in the case materials, bright students will infer a reasonable answer.

The changes in cash can be entirely explained by examining the changes in each of the other accounts on the balance sheet. This fact can be encouraging to students who are overwhelmed by the mechanics of preparing a cash flow statement. If each account on the balance sheet is taken in turn and the year over year change in that account is explained, the statement will balance.

Journal entries are used here to reinforce the connection between gain and loss transactions (such as the disposal of PP&E in this question) and the cash flow statement. The gross PP&E and the accumulated depreciation account are analyzed using T-accounts.

An approach that works well with this case is to have an overhead slide with the outline of the statement of cash flows. Students can be called on to fill in the numbers, explaining where they obtained the information and how they arrived at the amounts that go on the SCF.

There is one complication in the operating section of Frederick's statement of cash flows that deserves additional attention: the ESOP compensation add-back of $257. There are not sufficient details in the financial statements or the footnotes to allow the students to calculate the add-back. Therefore, we provide it to them. Background material is provided below to enable instructors to handle potential questions from students about this ESOP.

An Employee Stock Ownership Plan (ESOP) is a trusteed employee retirement benefit plan designed to invest primarily in "qualifying employer securities." It is a separate legal entity and may incur debt to purchase such securities in which event the plan is termed leveraged. In a leveraged ESOP, the trust borrows to acquire employer securities. The loan is guaranteed by the employer who makes annual contributions to the ESOP in amounts required to amortize the loan. The shares are held in a suspense account (a contra-equity account) and are released only as the debt is repaid.

In 1994, Frederick's established a leveraged ESOP for its employees and recorded the following journal entries:

Dr.   Reduction for ESOP loan guarantee:
("Unearned ESOP shares" contra-equity account)   960
Cr.   ESOP loan guarantee (liability)   960

It appears that annually, Frederick's is making contributions to the ESOP in order to amortize the ESOP loan liability. The 1996 financial statements show that two payments of $240 each, have been made.

In 1995 and 1996:
Dr.   ESOP loan guarantee (liability)   240
Cr.   Cash   240

Any interest incurred on this liability during the year would be charged to income as ESOP compensation. Frederick's financial statements indicate that total ESOP compensation for fiscal 1996 was $288,000 (more about this below). The outstanding liability of $480 appears on the balance sheet, part current ($240) and the rest long-term.

The shares acquired by the ESOP are held in a suspense account and are released for allocation to employees' individual accounts as the ESOP loan is repaid. Before ESOP shares are allocated to employees, however, Frederick's controls their use. Similarly, Frederick's controls how dividends paid on unallocated shares will be used. Frederick's may treat dividends on unallocated shares as direct compensation to employees who eventually are allocated the shares. In this instance, the dividends are to be recorded as a compensation expense. However, since the statement of cash flows shows the dividends on ESOP shares as a financing transaction, it is not clear if this is what Frederick's has done.

As shares are committed to be released, Frederick's will reduce the "Unearned ESOP shares" based on the cost of the shares to the ESOP. The difference between their original cost and the market value is to be charged or credited to additional paid-in capital.

Dr.   ESOP compensation   240
Dr.   Additional paid in capital   5
Cr.   Reduction for ESOP loan guarantee:
("Unearned ESOP shares" contra-equity account)   245

Note: During 1996, the additional paid in capital account changed from $438 to $432, a difference of $6. The journal entry differs by $1, this is likely due to rounding.

Compensation expense was also debited for other amounts likely for interest on the loan. The notes indicate that $288 was expensed during the year. Some of this was presumably paid in cash.

a. The Statement of Cash Flows (SCF) shows the cash that was provided from and used for the three main business activities: operations, investing, and financing. In contrast, the Income Statement (I/S) shows amounts related to operating activities (with few exceptions). Another important difference is that the SCF shows (indirectly) the cash actually *received* and *paid* during the one-year period; whereas the I/S shows amounts *earned* and costs *expensed* over the one-year period, regardless of when the cash was actually received or paid. This latter difference is due to the concept of "accrual accounting."

b. The two methods of preparing the Statement of Cash Flows are the indirect and the direct method. Frederick's uses the former. The statement begins with net income and reconciles that accrual figure to a cash-based income number "cash provided from operations."

c. The three sections of the Statement of Cash Flows are the operating section where net income determined on an accrual basis is reconciled to a cash-based equivalent, the investment section where the company's activities in asset acquisitions and divestitures are detailed, and the financing section which explains the uses and sources of cash related to the company's debt and equity financing. Interest expense is defined as an operating cash flow, dividends as a financing cash flow.

d. The three sections of the SCF are related to the balance sheet in a straightforward way. In general, the current assets and liabilities relate to cash from operations. Exceptions include marketable securities (which are investments) the current portion of long-term debt and lease obligations (which are financing cash flows). The long-term assets and changes in those accounts relate, for the most part, to the investing section. Fixed assets are the investments Frederick's makes to earn income. Last, the financing section is tied into the long-term debt section and the shareholders' equity section of the balance sheet. The "right hand side" of the balance sheet comprises the sources of funds Frederick's has tapped to finance its operations and its investment in long-term assets.

e. As disclosed in note 1, Frederick's considers, "highly liquid investments with an initial maturity of three months or less to be cash equivalents." This would include short-term commercial paper and 90 day certificates of deposit.

f. Net income is the *first* line item on Frederick's statement of cash flows (SCF) because the statement is prepared under the indirect approach. SCFs prepared under the direct approach do not have net income as the first line item. However, reconciliation of accrual-based net income with cash flows from operations is such an important concept that the FASB requires this reconciliation as a supplemental disclosure for firms using the direct approach (i.e., these firms disclose more than indirect-method firms).

Net income is reconciled with cash flows from operations because of the close relationship between the accounts in both sections. In general, items appearing in the operating section of the SCF are the same items that are used to compute accrual-based net income. The accruals outlined in the reconciliation help investors determine the quality of the company's earnings. Generally, earnings with a large proportion of accruals relative to cash flow are considered of lower quality.

g. i. Net income for the year was a loss of $438,000. This is the bottom line on the income statement. It becomes the first line on the SCF prepared using the indirect method.

g. ii. Because depreciation and amortization are not provided as a separate line item in the income statements, we need to find the information elsewhere. Note seven contains information on Frederick's segments. It is in this unlikely location that depreciation and amortization charges are disclosed. Retail stores recorded $3,758,000 in depreciation and catalog mail order recorded an additional $416,000 for a total provision of $4,174,000.

```
Dr.  Depreciation and amortization expense            4,174,000
Cr.       Accumulated depreciation and amortization              4,174,000
```
To record depreciation expense for the year.

g. iii. Capital expenditures are also disclosed in note seven. Totaling expenditures for the retail store and the catalog mail order we obtain expenditures of $4,073,000.

```
Dr.  Property and Equipment                           4,073,000
Cr.       Cash                                                   4,073,000
```
To record capital acquisitions during the year.

g. iv. The loss on disposal and on the write-down of the equipment is easily determined using T-accounts. The loss is $84,000.

(000's omitted)

Property and Equipment

Beg. Bal.	34,863		
Additions			Disposals
(note 7)	4,073	1,424	(plug)
End. Bal.	37,512		

Accumulated Depreciation

		16,638	Beg. Bal.
Disposals			Expense
(plug)	1,333	4,174	(note 7)
		19,479	End. Bal.

Using the information from the T-accounts above we can calculate the non-cash book loss on the disposal as follows:

Original cost of disposals	$ 1,424,000
Related accumulated depreciation	1,333,000
Net book value of disposals	91,000
Proceeds - given in question	7,000
Book loss (non-cash) on disposal	$84,000

```
Dr.  Cash                                                 7,000
Dr.  Accumulated Depreciation                         1,333,000
Dr.  Loss on sale of fixed assets                        84,000
Cr.       Property and Equipment                                 1,424,000
```
To record the sale of property and equipment at less than book value.

g. v. Frederick's balance sheet shows both deferred tax assets and deferred tax liabilities. The change in these two accounts combined can be used to infer the deferred tax expense for the year. The asset increased $78,000 and the liability decreased $8,000. This resulted in a non-cash deferred tax benefit on the income statement of $86,000. That is, the deferred tax accounts reduced tax expense for the year (increased the tax benefit) by $86,000.

```
Dr.  Deferred tax assets                                 78,000
Dr.  Deferred tax liability                               8,000
Cr.       Deferred tax expense                                      86,000
```
To record changes in the deferred tax accounts over the year.

h. Cash and equivalents — Changes in this account are the basis for the entire SCF. These changes do not appear in the operations section.

Accounts receivable — The accounts receivable outstanding at the end of the year are sales for which cash has not yet been collected. They must be deducted from accrual-based sales revenue to arrive at cash-based revenue. Similarly, the accounts receivable outstanding at the start of the year are not accrual-based sales. They must be added to accrual-based sales to arrive at cash-based revenue. This is algebraically equal to adding the $159,000 decrease in accounts receivable that happened during 1996.

Income tax receivable — Changes in this account relate to operations. The account has increased which means that Frederick's overpaid taxes. This was a use of cash. This $732,000 increase appears as a deduction in the operations section.

Merchandise inventories — Drawing down inventory generates cash. Thus, the $309,000 decrease in inventory means a source of cash that belongs in the operations section of the SCF.

Deferred income taxes — The increase in this asset arose because Frederick's recorded as reductions to tax expense amounts that DO NOT appear on their income tax return. It is a non-cash negative expense (akin to a benefit) and as such $78,000 needs to be deducted from accrual-based net income to arrive at cash from operations.

Prepaid expenses — Expenses paid in advance are related to operations that have been used up during the year. Therefore, the decrease in this account has been recorded as expense yet no cash has been used up. The $400,000 decrease in this account needs to be added back to reflect the non-cash expense charged to operations.

Accounts payable — The balance in this account indicates that some expenses recorded on the accrual basis have not yet been paid. On a cash basis, expenses are less by the unpaid amounts, that is, by the amounts in accounts payable at the end of the year. Likewise, the payables at the beginning of the year have been paid in cash by Frederick's during the year but not recorded as expenses. They were expenses the year before. The $1,319,000 decrease in the accounts payable balances (opening vs. closing) needs to be deducted in the operations section.

Dividends payable - This account is not related to operations but, rather, to financing.

Current portion of Capital lease obligations — This account is also related to financing.

ESOP loan guarantee — This account is also related to financing.

Accrued payroll — As with accounts payable, this account represents unpaid expenses at the end of the year. The account has decreased by $96,000 over the year which means that Frederick's paid, in cash, more than they recorded as expenses. They paid all their old bills and did not incur as much by the end of the year. This is a use of cash that appears in the operations section.

Accrued insurance — This is another accrual and like accrued payroll, this account decreased over the year. This $190,000 "use" of cash appears in the operations section.

Income taxes payable — During the year, Frederick's used cash to pay this tax bill. This will show up as a use of cash in the operations section of the SCF.

Other accrued expenses — This accrual is similar to the payroll accrual. It decreased over the year. The company paid all their old bills and did not incur as much by the end of the year. This decrease of $231,000 is a use of cash that appears in the operations section.

i. Statement of cash flows - operating section, see last page of solution.

j. In each of the past three years, cash from operating activities has been positive and has greatly exceeded net income. Unfortunately, the trend in cash flow from operations is downward. The company is having trouble remaining profitable (the segment disclosure note indicates that the problem lies more with the stores than the catalog operation).

Over the long run, cash flows from operating activities should exceed net income. This is because the cost of PP&E is an *investing* cash outflow but depreciation is an expense that is deducted from net income.

Cash flow from operations is often less than NI for high growth firms. They finance their increased levels of inventory and receivables with new debt or equity. But they eventually need to generate operating cash flow to pay off that debt. If a firm cannot generate sufficient operating cash flow in the long run, it will likely find that obtaining new capital (debt or equity) becomes very expensive (high interest rate or low price per share). Thus, it will likely cease to operate.

There is a direct relationship between cash flow from operations & investing and net income. In particular, over the life of an entity, the sum of cash flow from operations and cash flow from investing should equal the sum of net income. As such, net income can be used as an estimate of future cash flow from operations and investing. Of course, that assumes the past is representative of the future. The financial analyst's job is to draw on knowledge of current economic trends and company-specific events and combine that with historical financial statement data to forecast future cash flows and operating results.

k. Activity in the accounts receivable account is generally related to sales and collections made in the ordinary course of business. If a company has a net decrease in accounts receivable, it collected more cash from customers during the year than it generated in credit sales. This is what happened to Frederick's during fiscal year 1996. Because sales are positively related to net income, the excess of cash collections over (accrual basis) sales will be added to net income (the first line on the SCF) to determine cash flows from operations.

l. i.

Dr.	Retained Earnings (or Dividends Declared)	100
Cr.	Dividends Payable	100

To record dividends that were declared during the year.

l. ii. Because no cash changed hands before August 31, 1996, this amount would not be included in the financing section of the FY 1996 SCF. However, if the dividends are paid during fiscal year 1997, the FY 1997 SCF will include the $100 thousand as a financing use of cash.

m. i.

Dr.	Accounts Receivable	10,000
Cr.	Sales Revenue	10,000

To record additional 1996 sales.

m. ii. Because sales were understated by $10 million, income before tax is also understated by $10 million.

m. iii. This sales revenue relates to cash flows from operating activities. There is no effect on FY 1996 cash flows from operations because the increase in income (through sales) and the increase in accounts receivable will cancel each other out. The additional income tax expense that results from the increased sales will be offset by changes in the income tax payable and deferred tax accounts—again leading to no cash flow statement impact.

There is no impact on cash flows from investing activities because this transaction is related to operating activities.

FREDERICK'S OF HOLLYWOOD
CONSOLIDATED STATEMENTS OF CASH FLOWS

Cash flows from operating activities:	
Net income (loss)	$ (438)
Adjustments to reconcile net income (loss) to net cash from operations	
Depreciation and amortization (from segment information note 7, $3,758 + 416)	4,174
Deferred rent ($669 - 811)	142
Deferred income taxes (Asset increase $78, Liability decrease $8 Net use of cash $78 + 8)	(86)
ESOP non-cash portion of compensation ($288 - 31)	257
Loss on sale of fixed assets (See T-accounts above for analysis)	84
Changes in assets and liabilities: Accounts receivable ($658 - 499)	159
Income tax receivable ($945 - 213)	(732)
Merchandise inventories ($19,553 - 19,862)	309
Prepaid expenses ($2,215 - 2,615)	400
Accounts payable, ($10,298 - 11,617)	(1,319)
Accrued payroll ($430 - 526)	(96)
Accrued insurance ($828 - 1,018)	(190)
Other accrued expenses ($238 - 469)	(231)
Deferred catalog costs ($1,723 - 2,107)	384
Net cash provided by operating activities	$2,817

Fuji Photo Film & Eastman Kodak—Inferring Transactions

Teaching Notes:

This case complements the Yokohama and Goodyear case and introduces T-account analysis techniques. We provide a great deal of guidance for the T-account analyses. We have students set up T-accounts with opening and ending balances and then have them infer journal entries for each economic event. Those journal entries are used to fill in the account activity. In later cases, we provide much less guidance.

We also return to our comparison of debt-equity ratios across companies and countries. We provide a counterexample of the general finding that Japanese companies tend to have higher debt-equity ratios than U.S. companies (due to the close ties between banks and companies in Japan).

We use this case as a supplementary case at the beginning of the semester because, although we provide a good deal of guidance, many students find the account analysis aspects challenging.

a. i.

Dr.	Trade Accounts Receivable	¥1,437,810
Cr.	Net Sales	¥1,437,810

To record sales on account for Fuji Photo

a. ii.

Dr.	Cash	¥1,431,408
Cr.	Trade Accounts Receivable	¥1,431,408

To record collection of accounts receivable by Fuji Photo

The following T-account, in Japanese yen, is used to derive the journal entry for collections of trade receivables:

Trade Accounts Receivable

Beg Balance	234,068		
Sales	1,437,810	1,431,408	Collections (Plug)
End Balance	240,470		

b.

Dr.	Interest Expense	¥11,994
Cr.	Accrued Liabilities	¥11,994

To record accrued interest expense for Fuji Photo

c. i.

Dr.	Cost of Goods Sold	7,293
Cr.	Inventories	7,293

To record cost of goods sold for Eastman Kodak

c. ii.

Dr.	Inventories	7,465
Cr.	Payables	7,465

To record purchases on inventory on account for Eastman Kodak

c. iii.

Dr.	Payables	7,391
Cr.	Cash	7,391

To record payment for inventory purchased on account for Eastman Kodak

The following T-accounts are used to derive the journal entries in part c.

Inventories

Beg Balance	1,252		
Purchases (Plug)	7,465	7,293	COGS
End Balance	1,424		

Payables

		3,832	Beg Balance
Payments on account (Plug)	7,391	7,465	Purchases (from inventory T-account)
		3,906	End Balance

d.

Dr.	Research and Development Costs (Expense)	880
Cr.	Cash and or Short-term liabilities	880

To record research and development expense for Eastman Kodak

e.
Fuji Photo Film
Common-Size Income Statement
Years ended 1999 and 1998

	1999 ¥	1999 %	1998 ¥	1998 %
Net sales	1,437,810	100.0	1,378,061	100.0
Cost of sales	779,985	54.2	735,953	53.4
Gross profit	657,825	45.8	642,108	46.6
Operating Expenses:				
Selling, general and administrative	407,751	28.4	385,365	27.9
Research and development	84,740	5.9	81,043	5.9
Operating income	165,334	11.5	175,700	12.7
Other income and (expenses):				
Interest and dividend income	11,298	0.8	10,479	0.8
Interest expense	-11,994	-0.8	-11,524	-0.8
Exchange losses, net	-9,455	-0.6	-1,624	-0.1
Other, net	-17,972	-1.3	-10,578	-0.8
Income before taxes	137,211	9.5	162,453	11.8
Income taxes:				
Current	61,335	4.3	93,420	6.8
Deferred	11,276	0.8	-6,238	-0.5
	72,611	5.1	87,182	6.3
Income from consolidated companies	64,600	4.5	75,271	5.5
Equity in net earnings of affiliates	6,940	0.5	13,554	0.9
Net income	71,540	5.0	88,825	6.4

The common-size income statement shows that net income is almost one and a
half percent lower (as a percentage of revenues) in 1999 than in 1998. The
primary causes of this difference were increases in cost of goods sold (0.8%),
and a 0.5% increase in each of the following: selling, general and
administrative costs; other, net expenses; and foreign exchange losses. As
well, income from affiliates was down 0.4%. These decreases to net income were
partially offset by lower income tax costs (1.2%).

f. The debt-equity ratio can be calculated as total liabilities to total
shareholders' equity. In US dollars the ratios are:

$$\text{Fuji:} \quad \frac{3{,}691{,}050 + 391{,}430 + 812{,}818 + 447{,}421 + 169{,}141}{12{,}004{,}289} = 0.459$$

$$\text{Kodak:} \quad \frac{10{,}745}{3{,}988} = 2.53$$

This analysis indicates that Kodak is the more highly leveraged company.
Recall from the Yokohama Rubber & Goodyear Tire case that when comparing
ratios across domestic and foreign companies, it is important to be aware of
the business environment in which the companies operate. In that case, we
noted that Japanese companies tend to have higher debt/equity ratios because
of the strong ties between Japanese businesses and Japanese banks. In the case
at hand, a red flag is raised: the opposite relation is found. Thus, we should
investigate this further. Is Kodak over-leveraged? Is Fuji under-leveraged?

One reason that Kodak appears so highly leveraged is because the company has a
very large post-employment liability. It is Kodak's largest liability apart
from trade payables. However, this liability decreased during 1998 due to the
company's 1996 restructuring plan in which 17,400 jobs (along with health and
life insurance benefits) were eliminated. As well, recent aggressive stock

buy-backs have increased the level of treasury stock. During the second quarter of 1999, the Company completed stock repurchases under its 1996 $2 billion authorization. At 1998 year end, more than 17% of Kodak's issued stock is held in treasury (68 million treasury shares / 391 million shares issued = 17.4%). This reduces the denominator in the debt-equity ratio, above, thereby increasing the ratio.

One reason that Japanese companies are often heavily debt-financed has to do with post-W.W.II economic development practices. In many cases, the Japanese central government encouraged major banks to finance important industries. After the war, some of the prime targets for this policy were the major industrial companies. As an established company, Yokohama Rubber was likely the beneficiary of such policies. On the other hand, a company like Fuji which, arguably, operates in a less strategically important industry, may not have been targeted for heavy bank financing.

GTE—Persistence of Earnings

Teaching Notes:

This case illustrates the important concepts of the classified income statement and the persistence of earnings. GTE provides a nice example of the different categories of income: operating income, other income, discontinued operations, extraordinary items, and the cumulative effect of accounting changes. In addition, on the income statement, the company deducts preferred dividends to clearly illustrate what profits were earned by the common shareholders. Finally, the case ties in with the Maple Leaf Gardens case (valuation) and forces students to consider how straightforward valuation models need to be tailored for special circumstances—in this case, a company reporting losses.

a.   The major classifications used on the income statement are:

Operating income
Other revenues and expenses
Income from continuing operations before tax
Net income from continuing operations
Income or Loss from discontinued operations (net of tax)
Gain or loss on disposal of discontinued operations (net of tax)
Net income before extraordinary items
Extraordinary items (net of tax)
Net income before changes in accounting principle
Cumulative effect of change in accounting principle (net of tax)
Net income

Companies often disclose events separately within categories to draw further attention to them (for example, restructuring charges).

b.   According to the FASB's Statement of Concepts #5, "Effects of an entity's various activities, transactions, and events differ in stability, risk, and predictability, indicating a need for information about various components of earnings ... That need underlies the distinction between revenues and gains, between expenses and losses, between various kinds of gains and losses, and between measures found in current practice such as net income from continuing operations and net income." Thus, classified income statements help users better assess the persistence of earnings and the risk related to various components of net income.

c.   The GTE annual report provides an excellent example of why companies provide users with classified financial statements. The income statement reveals a number of nonrecurring items that should be evaluated if we want to estimate future earnings or cash flows. Generally accepted accounting principles require separate disclosure of a number of these items after income from continuing operations (e.g., discontinued operations, extraordinary items, cumulative effect of accounting changes). Notice that GTE voluntarily separated "Merger consummation and integration costs" in 1991. This was probably an attempt to signal to financial statement users that these costs would not recur in the future.

"Income from continuing operations" is probably the best proxy for future cash flows.

Note that although these classifications help users determine which components of earnings are "persistent" (or expected to recur), the distinction between categories is fuzzy. In addition, management normally has incentives to classify "good news" as related to continuing operations and "bad news" as unusual or non-recurring. The prudent reader of financial statements will endeavor to determine whether management's classifications are reasonable.

d.   Using income from continuing operations and the present value factor for an ordinary annuity for 40 years at 6.5%, the current value of the company is $14.7 billion.

($1,787 x 8.244 = $14,731 million)

e.   The market value (based on outstanding shares) of the company's common equity is $32.5 billion (i.e., 939,530,336 shares (945,147,187 - 5,616,851) at $34.63/share) at December 31, 1992.

Valuation of a company using discounted earnings is highly sensitive to growth rates and discount rates and number of periods as well as the estimate of residual value (i.e., what GTE could get for the net assets after it ceases operating). In this case, the market value of the company is greater than the discounted cash flow estimate of firm value. A likely reason is that the market is attributing a greater rate of growth to GTE's operations.

f.

	1992	1993	1994	1995	1996	1997	1998	1999	2000	2001 and beyond
Net Income	1,787	2055	2,363	2,718	3,125	3,594	4,133	4,753	5,466	62,561
Present value @ 12%		1,596	1,884	1,934	1,986	2,039	2,094	2,150	2,208	25,267
Value of equity	41,159	(sum of PVs)								
Common Shares	945,147,187									
Treasury Shares	5,616,851									
Outstanding Shares	939,530,336									
Price per share	$43.81									

NI for each of 1993 through 2000 is discounted at 12% per year.
The '2001 and beyond' term is determined as the present value of a growing perpetuity (5,466 * (1+.03)/(.12-.03)). This is discounted back to the end of 1992 at 12% for 8 periods.

The effect of growth on equity valuation is clear. Projecting 15% growth over the medium term and 3% growth thereafter, we arrive at a price almost 3 times as high as the initial valuation and 21% higher than the current market price. Of course, projecting earnings is as much an art as a science and requires in-depth knowledge of a company's competitive strategy and how its accounting data reflect the underlying economics. High quality accounting analysis allows analysts to assess the persistence of earnings and, thus, generate more accurate forecasts of future earnings.

The Home Depot—Long Term Debt

Teaching notes:

Home Depot has a variety of debt instruments that provide a nice way to discuss many of the more common debt features.

Students should understand the nature of different debt characteristics and be able to assess their impacts on future financial statements. In this case, students are presented the opportunity to see the impacts of a debt conversion versus a debt redemption.

Subsequent to year end, Home Depot offered to redeem their debt but, given the market price of the Home Depot stock, bondholders chose to convert to common stock at the expiry date (and not before). The last part of the case requires students to think about why debtholders would NOT convert their bonds to shares even though the "option" to convert is deep in the money. This can be used to start a discussion of risk preferences.

The Home Depot—Long Term Debt

a. Home Depot has $1,006,061 in long-term debt as of January 29, 1995. Of this, $22,692 is the current portion.

b. i. Commercial paper is short-term unsecured property notes issued by large corporations and finance companies. Typically, commercial paper expires in 270 days or less. It is a relatively cheap way to raise short term capital.

b. ii. According to SFAS #6, an entity may exclude a short-term obligation from current liabilities if both of the following conditions are met: 1) the entity must intend to refinance the obligation on a long-term basis; and 2) the entity must demonstrate an ability to consummate the refinancing. Based on the footnote, Home Depot has announced its intention to refinance the debt. The company's ability to refinance it is evidenced by the back-up credit facility it has arranged.

c. i. Convertible means that the notes can be exchanged or converted to common stock of Home Depot at the discretion of the noteholder.

c. ii. Subordinated implies that the notes are less senior than other debt issued by Home Depot. In the event that Home Depot were to declare bankruptcy, holders of the subordinated debt would be paid after the more senior claims are settled.

c. iii. Redeemable implies that Home Depot may repurchase or retire the notes on or before the maturity date.

d. i. The noteholders can either exchange each $1,000 note for $1,016.75 cash on March 31, 1995 or convert each $1,000 note into common shares of Home Depot on or before March 21, 1995. After that date, they have no choice, Home Depot will exercise their redemption option. The conversion price is $38.75 per share. Thus, each note can be converted to about 25.81 shares of common stock (i.e. $1,000/ $38.75 = 25.80645).

d. ii. The accrued interest is $5.50 per $1,000 note. If interest was last paid on the notes' anniversary date of February 15, 1995 then interest will accrue for 44 days before the redemption date, March 31. $1,000 x 4 1/2% x 44/365 = $5.50. Thus the redemption premium is $11.25 per note. ($16.75 - $5.50 = $11.25) Home Depot must pay this premium for the option of being able to redeem the notes.

d. iii. Each note has a face value of $1,000 and the total outstanding balance at year-end is $804,985,000. Thus, 804,985 notes are outstanding. Home Depot must issue 25.80645 shares per note. Therefore, if all the notes were converted Home Depot would need to issue 20,773,806 shares of common stock (per note two, approximately 20,774,000 shares).

e. i. If the market value of the stock was $36 then noteholders would **not** be inclined to exercise their conversion option. Doing so would mean the noteholders would pay $38.75 per share for something with a market value of $36. They would prefer the $1,016.75 cash from the redemption. Then, if they wanted to own Home Depot stock, they could use their redemption proceeds and buy stock on the open market for $36.

e. ii.

```
Dr.   Interest expense (804,985 x .045 x 44/365)        4,367
Dr.   Redemption premium  (plug)                        9,116
Dr.   4 1/2 % Notes (from B/S)                        804,985
Cr.          Cash (804,985 x 1.01675)                          818,468
```
To record redemption of notes for cash.

f. i. Because the market value of the stock was $44, noteholders would be inclined to exercise their option to convert their notes to stock at $38.75 per share. The conversion option is in the money. After exercise, noteholders could sell their stock on the open market for $44 and recoup $5.25 per share in profit.

f. ii.

```
Dr.   4-1/2 % Notes (from B/S)                        804,985
Cr.          Common stock - par (804,985 x 25.81 x .05 / 1000)   1,039
Cr.          Paid in Capital (plug)                            803,946
```
To record conversion of notes to common stock.

g. Noteholders may not have converted for several reasons. Some of them include:

- Ability to share in capital appreciation without owning the stock. If the note holders anticipate that Home Depot's stock price will rise, then waiting to convert will increase the option's value.
- Benefit from fixed returns on the note during the month before the conversion option expires.
- Better liquidity.

h.

```
Before:   2,335,818/3,442,223 = 0.6786
After:    (2,335,818-804,985)/(3,442,223+804,985)
          = 1,530,833/4,247,208 = 0.3604
```

After the conversion, Home Depot is less risky. The debt to equity measure tells us how much "buffer" a company has. A high debt to equity ratio implies that creditors' claims are large relative to available assets (claims may not be satisfied if Home Depot goes bankrupt), that the company is highly leveraged, and requires high cash flows to service the debt. In general, companies seek a ratio of between 1 to 1.5. Thus, Home Depot is not significantly risky before the conversion, but is less so afterwards.

i. Interest expense will decrease, all else being equal. The conversion of the notes to stock affects the balance sheet by changing debt into equity. In the future, interest expense will not include the 4-1/2% debt. With more shares outstanding, future EPS calculations will have a higher denominator.

Hydron Technologies Corporation—Lease or Buy

Teaching Notes:

This case allows students to apply present value concepts to a realistic business problem. Understanding present value and discounted cash flow concepts is particularly important but students sometimes don't see why it is covered in a financial accounting course—at least not until they cover topics such as long-term debt, leases, pensions, and valuation. We have found that it is useful to remind students why we cover present value in a financial accounting course. We introduce this topic early in the course because many topics require students' facility with PV concepts.

The key to solving this case is understanding the comparison that needs to be made. Many students do not see this immediately. Another area to watch out for is determining the correct discount rate. Many students will incorrectly apply the annual discount rate to each monthly period.

Hydron Technologies Corporation—Lease or Buy

a. A lease is a contractual arrangement where the lessor (who owns the asset) allows the lessee (who does not own the asset) to use or occupy the asset for a specified time in return for rent payments.

Leasing may be more advantageous than purchasing when:
- the lessee needs the asset for only a short time relative to the life of the asset
- the lessor is in a better position to sell the asset when it is no longer needed
- the lessee wants to avoid risks associated with technological obsolescence (i.e. the risk of resale prices being unexpectedly low)
- the lessee wants to avoid risks associated with potential environmental remediation
- the lessee does not want to report additional assets or liabilities on its balance sheet (i.e., to be able to report higher ROA or to avoid breaking restrictive debt covenants)
- it is to the lessee's advantage to deduct rent payments instead of interest and depreciation for tax purposes

Of course, the specific details of a given lease agreement can enhance or eliminate any of these advantages.

b. Virtually all kinds of equipment can be leased. If a company needs a machine for only a short period of time, it may choose to lease it rather than buy it (for example, a small landscape company might lease a cement mixer or a backhoe on an "as needed" basis; a larger company may find it more cost effective to own such equipment). On the other hand, some companies choose to lease assets that they know they will use for the life of the asset. Airlines are a case in point. They lease many of their aircraft. This allows them a degree of flexibility not available should they own the planes. They may also find that lessors offer competitive financing (i.e., interest) rates.

c. The way to solve this problem is to compare the $15,000 purchase price to the present value of the discounted lease payments and the "purchase option."

The lease payments to be discounted are:

3 years * 12 months	= 36	month lease term
First and last months' lease payments paid at inception	= (2)	
To be discounted	= 34	month "annuity in arrears"

The present value of the lease is computed as follows:

1. $305 annuity in arrears for 34 months
   at 8.5% / 12 = .7083% per month (see note below) $9,187

2. First and last months' payments made today
   ($305 + $305, not discounted)   610

3. Present value of $8,500 over 36 months at 8.5%
   (monthly compounding)— ($8,500 * $(1.007083)^{-36}$)   <u>6,593</u>

   Total Present Value   <u>$16,390</u>

Because the purchase price is less than the present value of the lease payments, it is cheaper to buy the computer than it is to lease it.

(An alternative way to determine the present value of the 36 payments of $305 is to determine the present value of an annuity DUE of 35 payments of $305 and add to that another $305—because two payments are made on signing the lease.)

d.   Some of the qualitative factors that need to be considered include:

- How will the lease affect reported earnings and solvency ratios? (Lease accounting is covered in a later case.)

- Does the company have $15,000 today?

- Technological obsolescence: the lease allows the company to "walk away" after three years. Buying does not.

- Who is responsible for insurance and maintenance?

NOTE: an annual discount rate of 8.5% compounded monthly is equivalent to a monthly discount rate of 8.5% / 12 = .7083%. This works out to an effective annual rate of $[(1 + .00783)^{12} -1] = 8.839\%$

Teaching Notes:

The direct method Statement of Cash Flows is easier to teach because it is more intuitive than the indirect method SCF. The operating section is the income statement prepared on a cash basis; line items correspond (although loosely) to the income statement. Few companies elect to use this method. The reasons are cost-related, yet a few firms, such as Jan Bell, continue to use the direct method.

The FASB's SFAS No. 95 requires that a reconciliation of net income to cash flow from operations be included if the direct method is used. That portion of Jan Bell's statement of cash flows can be tied into the requirements of the case. Individual items are, however, difficult to reconcile. We illustrate the general relationship between the direct and indirect method SCF by reconciling the cash collected from customers with sales and the change in accounts receivable. We ask students to identify (but not reconcile) the balance sheet changes that tie into cash paid to suppliers and employees.

Reconciling the accrual (income statement) amounts to their cash based equivalents in this way is an excellent way to demonstrate interactions between balance sheet and income statement items. Students with no accounting background tend to decouple the two statements. Many control and financial reporting issues can be more easily understood by simultaneously examining the issue in the context of both statements. This case helps build that skill.

a. Jan Bell Marketing Inc. uses the direct method of preparing their statement of cash flows. Each line item in the operations section is similar to a cash-based income statement. Had they used the indirect approach, the more common approach, the operations section of the statement of cash flows would have started with net income and reconciled that accrual-based number to a cash-based number.

FASB Standard No. 95 provides that either of the two methods can be used to report "cash flows from operating activities." The only difference in the two methods lies in the preparation of the operating activities section. In the direct method, all cash flow activities from operations are reported. With the indirect method, all operating non-cash adjustments are added or subtracted from net income to arrive at "net cash flows from operations." The end result under each method is identical.

b. There are two cost-related reasons most companies use the indirect approach. First, the cost of producing "direct" information can be much higher. For example, all cash flows would have to be separately identified as operating, investing, or financing. The additional expense of reprogramming a company's bookkeeping and accounting-information system could outweigh the benefit of providing the information. Second, the indirect method information is included in the reconciliation at the bottom of the direct method statement. Including this information creates additional cost to produce direct-method SCF.

c. i.

Dr.	Depreciation and Amortization Expense	8,704	
Cr.	"Assets"*		8,704

To record deprecation and amortization for 1996.

*It is difficult to isolate which assets were depreciated or amortized in 1996. There would certainly have been depreciation on the "Property" and amortization of the "Excess of cost over the fair value of assets acquired" (i.e., goodwill). There may also have been depreciation or amortization charged against "Other assets" and "Other current assets." As the account titles are not descriptive, it is difficult to say how much with certainty. Below, we estimate the portion of the $8,704 attributable to various line items.

Depreciation of PPE = Net Property (beginning) + Capital expenditures (SCF) - Net Property (ending) = 29,639 + 1,826 - 25,943 = $5,522

Amortization of Goodwill - Excess of cost over the fair value of assets acquired (beginning) - Purchased Goodwill - Excess of cost over the fair value of assets acquired (ending) = 2,869 + 0 - 2,685 = 184

Unexplained depreciation and amortization: 8,704 - 5,522 - 184 = 2,998

c. ii. Depreciation is added to net loss (i.e., reduces to negative balance) to arrive at cash flow from operations because it is an expense that does not use cash. That is, cash is spent when PPE is paid for, not when PPE is depreciated. On an indirect statement of cash flows, the first item listed is net income (or loss). That figure includes a deduction for depreciation expense. By adding depreciation back to net income (or loss), the end result is to adjust net income to exclude the non-cash charge.

Depreciating more in a given year would lead to a lower net income figure and a correspondingly higher depreciation add back. There would be no net effect on cash flow from operations.

d.   The accrual-based measure "Net sales" ties into "Cash received from customers" (the amount on the direct method SCF) by considering the net change in accounts receivable. Receivables decreased during the year. This means that Jan Bell received more cash from its customers than it recorded as sales for 1996. Consequently, the indirect method SCF adds the decrease in A/R to Net Income—which implicitly incorporates "Net sales"—to arrive at the cash collected from customers.

Net sales ($254,004) plus the decrease in Accounts receivable ($6,301) is virtually identical to the amount reported as Cash received from customers ($260,304 per the SCF). The $1 difference is likely due to rounding.

e.   For a retailer, the cash equivalent of cost of sales is the amount paid to suppliers (as shown on the direct method SCF). This amount can be arrived at by starting with cost of sales—an outflow implicitly listed on an indirect SCF as a component of net income—and subtracting (adding) the net increase (decrease) in inventory and adding (subtracting) the net increase (decrease) in accounts payable. (This assumes that only purchases of inventory run through accounts payable.)

For manufacturers such as Jan Bell, the picture is more complex. The change in inventory will incorporate not only purchases of raw materials, but also allocations of direct and indirect labor and manufacturing overhead. Consequently it is usually not possible for external users of the Financial Statements to derive a "pure" cash-basis equivalent for cost of sales. At Jan Bell, the SCF includes "cash paid to suppliers and employees." This outflow is the cash-basis equivalent of "Cost of sales," "Store and warehousing operating and selling expenses," and "General and administrative expenses" for fiscal 1996.

L.A. Gear, Inc.—Cash and Balance Sheet Issues

Teaching Notes:

Students find this case appealing because they are familiar with the Company. What students tend to find surprising is that L.A. Gear experienced some cash constraints during 1992 which started as early as 1989. Bank of America's requirement of dollar for dollar collateralization of letters of credit speaks to their opinion of L.A. Gear's credit worthiness.

The use of standby and commercial letters of credit is increasing. Most large banks carry these financial instruments on their balance sheets and as international trade increases, we will see them more frequently on other corporate balance sheets as well.

Students are sometimes intimidated by the heavily crafted notes to the financial statements. Explaining the accounting jargon in plain English is a useful exercise.

L.A. Gear, Inc.—Cash and Balance Sheet Issues

a. i. The collateralized cash referred to in the note is cash earmarked as collateral for outstanding letters of credit. Letters of credit are letters or documents issued by a bank authorizing a named person to obtain a specified amount of money from the bank's branches or correspondents. It is probable that this credit arrangement facilitates L.A. Gear in their cash and credit needs, particularly in the payment of foreign suppliers.

For example, L.A. Gear has suppliers in Asia who may not readily accept checks drawn on L.A. Gear's US bank accounts. L.A. Gear arranges with the Bank of America to have the Bank of America pay the suppliers directly (likely through one of the Bank of America's correspondent banks in Asia). When L.A. Gear orders inventory from their supplier, the Bank of America issues a letter of credit to the supplier and effectively provides the supplier with assurance that the supplier will be paid by Bank of America.

Two things are worth noting. First, as at the balance sheet date L.A. Gear has only ordered inventory. Bank of America has collateralized the cash so L.A. Gear shows that. However, the company has not set up an asset for the inventory or a payable for the amount due to Bank of America. Typically, companies record the inventory transaction when they receive the goods. Second, it seems that L.A. Gear's bank does not have much confidence in the company's solvency as they take an extreme position and require that each dollar available through the outstanding letters of credit be matched with collateralized cash. This helps ensure that the bank will be repaid by L.A. Gear and that it won't end up with a boatload of sneakers.

a. ii. The line of credit in the 1991 financial statements is revolving. L.A. Gear draws upon it to meet unspecified cash needs. It is an agreement by the bank that allows L.A. Gear to spend more cash than their checking account balance indicates—essentially it is an overdraft arrangement. At November 30, 1991, L.A. Gear had drawn upon this revolving credit facility for a total of $20 million.

A letter of credit is a different arrangement. The bank stands ready to meet specified cash needs. There are several kinds of "letters of credit." While they all, in general, substitute the bank's credit rating for L.A. Gear's they differ in other respects. A "Standby Letter of Credit" is a letter of credit where a bank pays a supplier only if the bank's customer does not fulfill its obligation to pay the supplier directly. That is, if L.A. Gear had a standby letter of credit facility, then L.A. Gear would be expected to pay its suppliers directly. If it didn't, then the Bank of America would pay the supplier and then go after L.A. Gear. In the ordinary course of business, banks do not anticipate drawing down a standby.

"Commercial Letter of Credit" is an arrangement where the bank agrees to pay the supplier directly--typically when provided with evidence that goods have been shipped. The bank fully expects, under normal business circumstances, to honor the commercial letter of credit. This seems to be the type of letter of credit that L.A. Gear has with the Bank of America.

As an aside, you might have seen accounts called "Banker's acceptance" in a set of financials before. This relates to letters of credit. If the bank pays the supplier in, say, 30 days, then the bank has issued a "Banker's Acceptance" to the supplier to cover the interim period. After paying the supplier, the bank then notifies its customer (i.e., L.A. Gear) and the customer pays the bank.

a. iii. The difference is likely a "compensating balance" required by the Bank of America in return for the letter of credit facility. This represents the fee L.A. Gear must pay for having the facility available. The effect of this compensating balance (which may not be available for general use) on the working capital position of L.A. Gear is minor.

b. Current assets and liabilities are 230,100 and 62,051, respectively.

Working Capital = Current Assets - Current Liabilities.

Working Capital @ 11/30/92 = 230,100 - 62,051 = 168,049.

c. Current Ratio = Current Assets/Current Liabilities.
(Also referred to as the "working capital ratio.")

Current Ratio @ 11/30/92 = 230,100/62,051 = 3.71.

Quick Ratio = Quick Assets/Current Liabilities.
Quick assets are usually defined as cash, marketable securities and accounts receivable. Quick assets represent the most liquid assets a firm has.

Quick Assets @ 11/30/92 = (55,027 + 28,955 + 56,369) = 140,351.
Quick Ratio @ 11/30/92 = 140,351/62,051 = 2.3.

d. Working capital (the excess of current assets over current liabilities) represents L.A. Gear's ability to meet maturing short-term obligations. The working capital ratio (or current ratio) measures the same thing except in quotient form. A ratio greater than 1.0 indicates an ability to meet current obligations. The working capital ratio is very useful when considered with other measures of liquidity and when compared with historical and industry averages.

The quick ratio measures the ability to meet immediately maturing obligations. Accounts receivable are typically included in the measure of quick assets. However, if there is doubt about the L.A. Gear's ability to collect these amounts quickly, they should be left out of the calculation.

L.A. Gear appears to be in a position to meet its current obligations.

e. One might argue that although the collateralized cash is classified as current on the balance sheet, it is not part of working capital because is it not available to satisfy current obligations. Therefore, the current ratio could be recalculated as follows: (230,100 - 28,955)/62,051 = 3.24

However, this represents only a partial analysis. When the letter of credit is drawn down (which means, when Bank of America pays the supplier) what journal entry will L.A. Gear make? Drawdown will occur only when the supplier has provided Bank of America with evidence that the goods have been received by L.A. Gear. L.A. Gear's entry will be, in thousands:

Dr.	Inventory	28,800	
Dr.	Bank fees (an expense)	155	
Cr.	Collateralized cash		28,955

To record drawdown of the letter of credit.

Therefore, there is a reduction to current assets of only 155. If the event will occur with relative certainty, the working capital and current ratio are affected but not by a material amount.

For its part, the quick ratio IS materially affected if collateralized cash is taken into account. Quick assets are reduced by the entire amount, $28,955 to $111,396.

Quick Ratio (recalculated) @ 11/30/92 = 111,396/62,051 = 1.8.

Lands' End, Inc.—Inventory

Teaching Notes:

In this case, students learn about different cost flow assumptions and how to convert from one to the other. They perform T-account analysis in the process. That important tool is a fundamental one that we return to over and over in these cases.

The case also helps students understand why many balance sheet changes do not tie in directly to the statement of cash flows. This issue is one many students struggle with and so it is appropriate to spend additional time explaining why it arises.

Finally, the case includes a *Wall Street Journal* article that comments on Lands' End's inventory position. Students infer from the article why an increase in inventory is considered bad news and they consider the importance of timely and open communication between analysts and companies.

Lands' End, Inc.—Inventory

a.   Companies use cost flow assumptions to cost their inventory because in most cases, it would be prohibitively expensive to track individual units of inventory. Imagine the problems associated with tracking individual pairs of jeans at Lands' End's warehouse, or hardware items at Home Depot. Of course, for low volume, high price goods such as automobiles or jewelry, the cost of tracking individual items is more than offset by the benefits of specific identification.

Lands' End uses the Last In, First Out method of inventory costing.

b.   If prices are increasing and the company is not reducing the level of inventory it holds, then compared to the FIFO method, the LIFO method leads to lower balance sheet values for inventory, higher income statement values for cost of goods sold, and no DIRECT difference on the statement of cash flows. Cash flow (i.e., payments for inventory) is completely unrelated to how inventory is costed. There is an indirect cash flow effect, however. If companies are allowed to use LIFO for tax purposes, then taxable income will be lower (under the above assumptions) and so income tax payments will be lower. (When the company is liquidated and the inventory eventually disposed of, it will generate relatively low cost of goods sold and a higher tax bill.)

c.   The two numbers differ due to the effect of acquiring other businesses during fiscal 1995 (see note 8). When Lands' End acquires other businesses it acquires their inventory (and cash and receivables, etc.). That, of course, leads to a change in the inventory account. However, on the SCF the acquisition (including the related inventory) is included under the investment section and not the operations section.

d. i.

Inventory			
Beginning balance	149,688		
Purchases (plug)	587,598	568,634	Cost of Goods Sold
Ending balance	168,652		

Dr. Inventory	587,598		
Cr. Accounts Payable		587,598	
To record purchase of inventory			

d. ii.

	Accounts Payable		
		54,855	Beginning balance
Payments (plug)	589,691	587,598	Purchases (see above)
		52,762	Ending balance

Dr. Accounts Payable	589,691		
Cr. Cash		589,691	
To record payment			

e.

	Inventory (FIFO)		
Beginning balance	149,688 + 19,100		
Purchases (c. i.)	587,598	568,834	Cost of Goods Sold
Ending balance	168,652 + 18,900		

In the above T-account we have filled in the information needed to adjust Lands' End's inventory to a FIFO basis. We used information from Note 1 to adjust the opening and ending balances, and information from part c. i. to determine purchases. Remember, purchases are unaffected by the choice of inventory cost flow—they simply represent the stack of invoices received for inventory acquired. Cost of goods sold is the plug. We then adjust the income statement for the restated COGS, use the average tax rate reported to adjust income tax expense and arrive at adjusted net income.

Net income before tax as reported	$ 59,663	
Add LIFO COGS	568,634	
Less FIFO COGS	568,834	
NIBT Restated	59,463	
Income tax at reported rate	23,488	(23,567 / 59,663 = 39.5%)
Net income (restated)	$ 35,975	

In contrast with the discussion in part b, net income at Lands' End is higher under LIFO than FIFO. This could be due to lower inventory costs on new inventory. However, Lands' End reported that its inventory costs rose slightly in fiscal 1995.

A more likely, and more complex, reason involves the company's LIFO pools. The company pools certain types of inventories, each of which is accounted for using LIFO. Suppose one of these pools was made up of old styles and had a relatively large "LIFO reserve." If the company liquidated that merchandise, that part of the LIFO reserve would be gone and might more than offset the increase in the difference between LIFO and FIFO (i.e., the LIFO reserve) that occurred in other pools.

f. The cumulative effect of using LIFO (instead of FIFO) shows up in the ending LIFO Reserve. Because Lands' End used LIFO, the additional cost of goods sold they have reported (not just this year, but since the start-up of the company) is $18,900. The tax savings they have achieved by having this higher tax deduction are $18,900 * 39.5% (the company's average tax rate) = $7,466. The estimated savings would be higher (or lower) if tax rates in prior years were higher (lower) than this years' average rate. Of course, eventually, the company will have higher profits and have to pay additional taxes (i.e., when the company liquidates its "low cost" LIFO inventory) but that time may be in the indefinite future. In addition, that liquidation might only take place if the company was in dire straights and losing money. In that case, income taxes might not arise.

g. i. The analysts are concerned about the increase in inventory at Lands' End because it may be a signal that the company has surplus inventory. If that is the case, it may have to liquidate the goods at lower than normal profits. In addition, holding the inventory is costly. It leads to higher interest costs (more money has to be borrowed to finance the inventory), higher bookkeeping costs, higher insurance costs, the cost of additional warehouse space, and so on.

Of course, the company explains this differently. They maintain that the increase was by design. They are attempting to ship 90% of their orders on the day of the order. That means they need to have the goods in stock.

g. ii. It is important for companies to communicate regularly and openly with shareholders and analysts because not doing so can lead to swings in stock prices as analysts jump to conclusions (often negative) when they are surprised. The WSJ article outlines such a case. Analysts don't want to have buy recommendations out on a stock only to find that there is bad news lurking. Frequent and open meetings create an atmosphere of trust that can ultimately lead to a lower cost of capital for the firm.

Maple Leaf Gardens—Valuation

Teaching Notes:

This case offers students the opportunity to value a company. We make a number of simplifying assumptions, but in class discussion instructors should encourage students to challenge the assumptions and discuss how better figures could be arrived at. The case illustrates the important differences between book and market values. It also illustrates the difference between balance sheet and income statement-based valuation approaches.

An active learning approach to this case involves splitting the class into three types of subgroups: buyers, sellers, and arbitrators. Have each group work independently to arrive at a valuation (the arbitrators can determine what they feel is a "fair" price). Then have the subgroups negotiate (in larger classes, several sets of negotiations can take place). Finally have the groups report to the class.

a. i. Molson's assets, liabilities, revenues and expenses are excluded from the financial statements of Maple Leaf Gardens Ltd. (MLG) (as are the assets, etc. of all other shareholders). Normally, an owner's (e.g., Molson's) assets could not be used to satisfy creditors of the company, nor would other profits earned by Molson's accrue to other shareholders. Consequently, under the economic entity assumption of GAAP, financial statements report on individual economic entities, separate from their owners.

a. ii. The fiscal period assumption of financial reporting implies that the life of an economic entity can be divided into arbitrary time periods. Most often, the time period is one calendar year. Some companies choose year ends to match the end of their business cycle. For example, many retailers use January 31 year ends, allowing them to report holiday sales revenues for the period. Other companies choose year ends to maximize tax benefits available. For example, in some jurisdictions, companies can claim tax credits based on the level of inventory they hold at year end. That would prompt retailers to have pre-holiday year ends because that is when their inventories peak. MLG has a May 31 year end. Typically this would fall right after the end of the hockey season. Thus, all ticket and advertising revenue for a given hockey season would have been earned.

a. iii. If a company uses accrual-basis accounting, it records the effects of economic events as the events occur and not as cash (or its equivalent) is received or paid. The latter is cash-basis accounting.

MLG uses accrual-basis accounting—an assumption underlying GAAP. For example, MLG records wage expense as wages are earned regardless of whether employees are paid in advance or will be paid in some future year.

a. iv. The going concern assumption is perhaps the most critical assumption underlying accrual accounting. Invoking the assumption, one assumes that the entity will operate beyond the current year, indefinitely into the future. The going concern assumption must be met whenever a company capitalizes costs. For example, MLG capitalizes "deferred charges" which represent initial signing bonuses for some players. Rather than expense these costs immediately, they are capitalized and amortized over the players' contract periods. If the company was not expected to operate in the future, there would be no basis for calling such costs assets and allocating them over the players' contract periods. In other words, there would be no expected future economic benefit. Thus, the going concern assumption is critical to the matching principle (the basis for accrual accounting).

a. v. There are numerous examples of the matching principle on the MLG Financial Statements.
- Building and Equipment: costs are capitalized and depreciated over their useful lives. This "matches" their costs with the revenues they generate.
- Deferred Charges: these represent signing bonuses paid to hockey players. They are capitalized initially and amortized over the term of the contracts. This "matches" the cost of player salaries with the annual ticket revenue.
- Deferred Income: this represents advance ticket sales. As such, they represent future liabilities. When the games are played or events held, MLG will recognize revenue and "match" it with the costs associated with the game or event.
- On the I/S, we see that operating revenues for a period are matched with operating expenses for the period.

a. vi.   Revenue recognition refers to the time or event that triggers a company to record revenue in its books. The decision can be tricky. For example, MLG sells tickets in advance of the playing of hockey games. Should it record a "sale" when a season ticket holder pays for a whole season's worth of tickets? Should MLG wait until ALL the games are played before recording a sale? Should MLG recognize revenues on a game by game basis? If MLG records revenue when a season ticket order is received, how should it treat cases where season ticket holders pay in installments?

Revenue recognition criteria help in this regard. According to the FASB's conceptual framework (Statement of Concepts No. 5: Recognition and Measurement in Financial Statements of Business Enterprises), revenues are "… generally not recognized until realized or realizable. Revenues … are realized when products (goods or services), merchandise, or other assets are exchanged for cash or claims to cash. Revenues … are realizable when related assets received or held are readily convertible to known amounts of cash or future claims to cash. Revenues are not recognized until earned. An entity's revenue-earning activities involve delivering or producing goods, rendering services, or other activities that constitute its ongoing major or central operations, and revenues are considered to have been earned when the entity has substantially accomplished what it must do to be entitled to the benefits represented by the revenues. …"

In plain English, this means revenue should be recognized when the entity has performed all or a significant portion of the work it expects to perform and that the entity can reasonably measure the cash, receivable, or other form of payment it will receive.

In the case of MLG, they recognize revenue for events after the events have taken place. They recognize revenue for merchandising and concession sales as those sales take place. If MLG licenses the Toronto Maple Leaf team logo to merchandisers, revenue should be recognized according to the terms of the contract. If the contract calls for a fee based on the merchandiser's sales, then revenue would be recognized as those sales take place. If there is a fixed fee component to the sale, the fee should be recognized as revenue either over the term of the contract (if MLG has any associated obligations to perform) or immediately (if MLG has no remaining obligations to the licensee).

b. i.   The net book value (NBV) of MLG at May 31, 1992 is $15,134,800 (Cdn). This amount is the difference between the assets and liabilities of the company. NBV is analogous to the equity a homeowner has in his/her house calculated by comparing the *purchase* price of the home and the current mortgage balance. Note that NBV is not likely to be the same as the "fair market value" of the company, which is based on present day asset and liability values or the future earnings of the firm.

b. ii.   Generally, current assets and liabilities are stated at close to fair market value. One important exception is inventory, but MLG has none. Fixed assets represent the company's land, building, and equipment and are stated at their original cost to the company less depreciation. Depreciation, in accounting, is a means of allocating the original cost of an asset to the periods that benefit from its use. It is not a means of valuing an asset. Therefore, there's a good chance that the FMV of the fixed assets is different than their NBV—especially because Maple Leaf Gardens (the hockey arena, not the company) sits on expensive real estate in downtown Toronto.

Deferred Charges, per note 1, represent signing bonuses to Toronto Maple Leaf hockey players. It's much like a prepaid rent or insurance account for companies in more "traditional" industries. This is a hard one to value. Indeed, what is the value of "hockey talent" for an NHL team?

Deferred Income Taxes (Debit) represent the excess of the amount which MLG has paid Revenue Canada (the Canadian equivalent of the Internal Revenue Service) over the amount it has charged to Income Tax Expense. As we will see in later cases, we calculate Income Tax Expense on accounting income (or the GAAP value of assets and liabilities) and Income Tax Payable on taxable income (or the tax value of assets and liabilities) and the two measures are rarely the same in a given year. Valuing deferred tax assets and liabilities is tricky and is left to advanced accounting courses.

The final asset is the NHL franchise fee. MLG is carrying this asset on its books at only $100,001. This seems very low, especially in light of Note 3. Note 3 explains that when the Ottawa, Tampa Bay, and San Jose franchises joined the NHL in 1991, they paid $50,000,000 (U.S.). It seems reasonable that other franchises are worth that much, too. (On May 26, 1995, the *Toronto Star* reported that the Quebec Nordiques hockey franchise had been sold for U.S. $75 million and was being moved to Denver, Colorado.)

Liabilities are generally assumed to have NBVs that approximate FMV. This assumption may not always hold, however, if a company has long-term debt (e.g., bonds) during periods of fluctuating interest rates. As all of MLG's liabilities are current, it is reasonable to assume that NBV approximates FMV.

b. iii.

Accounts	As Stated (NBV)	Adjusted (FMV)
Current Assets	6,675,811	6,675,811
Land	358,811	2,392,073
Building and Equipment	12,626,405	12,626,405
Deferred Charges	1,400,428	1,400,428
Deferred Income Tax	468,980	468,980
Franchise ($1 Cdn = $.75 U.S.)	100,001	66,666,666
Liabilities	(6,495,636)	(6,495,636)
Net value of MLG	15,134,800	83,734,727

b. iv. The difference between the amounts in parts b(i) and b(iii) is attributable to the appreciation in value of individual assets. If the company were to sell the individual assets of MLG, we would expect a gain equal to the difference between the net FMV and the NBV.

c. i. $15.38 = 1 / r$

$r = 6.5\%$

This rate seems very low. It is only slightly above the rate paid by long-term government bonds—and those bonds are substantially less risky.

On the other hand, the low rate compensates for the fact that no growth in earnings was factored in (see below).

c. ii. Using the PE multiple of 15.38 and net income from continuing operations, we arrive at a value of $110,248,223 (i.e., 15.38 * $7,168,285).

Using net income from continuing operations we are implicitly assuming that MLG will continue to receive franchise revenue each year. This does not seem reasonable. There are a limited number of cities that could support an NHL team. As such, the franchise fee revenues are not as persistent as the other revenues. In addition, we are not allowing for possible work stoppages, lockouts, or strikes. A lockout interrupted the 1994-95 season forcing the cancellation of almost half the regular season games and the loss of substantial ticket and advertising revenues.

c. iii. $15.38 = (1 + g) / (r - g)$

If $r = 15\%$, then $g = 7.98\%$

We could assess whether the growth rate was reasonable by looking at past growth rates for MLG and other hockey franchises. We also could look to industry trends and expansion plans announced by the NHL.

A growth rate of 7.98% for an infinite period seems unreasonable. Competition from other sources (i.e., other sports) will drive the rate down in the long run. In practice, analysts attempt to project growth until a competitive equilibrium is reached and then forecast no real growth for future years.

c. iv. The difference between b(iii) and c(ii) represents the value of MLG's assets taken together. That is, owning a parcel of land in downtown

Toronto, the only professional sports arena, and an NHL franchise is worth more than the sum of the individual assets (i.e., land, arena, franchise) owned by three unrelated companies. If MLG was bought by another entity for the amount in part c(ii) and the transaction was accounted for using "purchase" accounting, the difference between b(iii) and c(ii) would be set up as an asset called "goodwill."

d. A good estimate of the FMV of MLG is based on an arm's-length exchange between two independent parties. The April 5, 1994 *Wall Street Journal* article describes such a proposed exchange. Based on the 49% stake to be purchased by the Ontario Teacher's pension fund, the company is worth $124,490,000 (Cdn) ($61,000,000 / .49). Note that this figure is approximately equal to the $125,000,000 total value of the takeover offer discussed in the article.

The differences in the value calculated based on the WSJ article and the discounted cash flow analysis could stem from a number of sources. For example, perhaps our implied discount rate was too high (this seems unlikely, 6.5% is rather low). Alternatively, Steve Stavro may have plans for MLG that differ from those the company is presently pursuing.

Teaching Notes:

This case puts present value in an equity security investment setting. The problem walks students through the basic calculations. Gradually, the questions get more difficult. The notion that an investment grows through time is intuitive to most students. The case starts with that notion (part b).

The notion that the value of a dollar in the future is worth less than the value of the dollar today is less intuitive. The second part of the case demonstrates this concept over a number of time period and cash flow assumptions. Thus, the case builds in the compounding concept.

Using a time line to demonstrate these concepts has proven successful in the classroom.

Maya, Inc.—Return on Investment

a. i. Most people would say that $100 today is more valuable than $100 in the future. The reason is that if you had the $100 today, you could consume it. The value of consumption today is generally considered higher than consumption in the future—especially if you expect inflation to erode the "real" value of the $100 in the future. Alternatively, you could invest it and end up with more than $100 in the future.

a. ii. A lump sum payment is a single payment (as opposed to a series of payments).

a. iii. An annuity is a series of payments. The payments are equal in amount and equally spaced in time. In the case of an ordinary annuity, the first payment is made one "period" from today. For example, bonds pay interest at the end of every six month period. In the case of an annuity due, the first payment is made today. For example, you probably pay rent to your landlord at the beginning of the month.

a. iv. *Simple* interest means interest is earned only on the principle, whereas *compound* interest means interest is earned on both principle and unpaid interest. To illustrate, assume you borrowed $100 for two years at 10% annual *simple* interest. At the end of the two years, you will owe $120: the original $100 plus $10 (i.e., $100 * 10%) for each year you had the loan. If the loan was at 10% *compounded* annually, at the end of the two years you would owe $121. You would owe $110 ($100 plus $10 of interest) after the first year and an additional $11 of interest ($110 * 10%) for the second year. The extra dollar represents interest on the interest that had accrued by the end of the first year but had not yet been paid.

a. v. The return on a share of stock is:

(change in share price + dividends) / beginning share price

Note that this does not take into account the length of time over which the change in price occurred or the timing of the dividend payments. The tools you need to apply are discussed in the following parts of the case.

b. i. You would earn 12% if after one year the share price was:

$45 + $45 * (.12) or $45 * (1 + .12) = $50.40.

b. ii. To earn 12% compounded annually over two years, you would need to earn an additional 12% on the balance accumulated through the end of the first year. That would be

[$45 * (1 + .12)] * (1 + .12) or $45 * (1 + .12)^2 = $56.45.

b. iii. To earn 12% compounded annually over five years, you would need to earn an additional 12% on the balance accumulated through the end of each year. That would be

$45 * (1 + .12)^5 = $79.31.

Notice how the three problems all boil down to applying the following formula:

$$FV = PV * (1 + i)^n$$

where FV is future value, PV is present value, i is the periodic interest rate and n is the number of periods (note that i and n are defined over the same time period, for example, both are in years or both are in months).

c. Using the formula $FV = PV * (1 + i)^n$, we can solve for the realized return as follows:

$$5,000 = 4,500 * (1 + i)^5 \text{ or } 1.11111 = (1 + i)^5$$

Using a calculator we can solve for i, in this case 2.13%.

Alternatively, we could use a future value table. Looking across the row n = 5 we would find that the factor 1.1111 lies between 2% and 3%.

d. i. Rearranging the terms in the future value formula we get:

$$PV = FV * (1 + i)^{-n}$$

In this case, $PV = 5,000 * (1 + .12)^{-1} = \$4,464.29$ or $44.64 per share.

d. ii. Two years out we get:

$$PV = 5,000 * (1 + .12)^{-2} = \$3,985.97 \text{ or } \$39.86 \text{ per share.}$$

d. iii. Five years out we get:

$$PV = 5,000 * (1 + .12)^{-5} = \$2,837.13 \text{ or } \$28.37 \text{ per share.}$$

d. iv. In this case, rather than receiving $5,000 in one year, you get $5,000 + 100 * $4.50 or $5,450. The present value of which is:

$$PV = 5,450 * (1 + .12)^{-1} = \$4,866.07 \text{ or } \$48.66 \text{ per share.}$$ Notice that the dividend of $4.50 does not increase what you would be willing to pay by $4.50. Rather, the increase is $4.02 ($48.66 - $44.64)—the present value of $4.50 (at 12% one period hence).

d. v. The best way to solve this problem is to draw a time line.

```
?
|-------+-------+-------+-------+-------|
       450     450     450     450   450 + 5,000
```

We could find the present value of each of the six payments one at a time. That comes to:

$$450 * (1.12)^{-1} = \$401.79$$
$$450 * (1.12)^{-2} = \$358.74$$
$$450 * (1.12)^{-3} = \$320.30$$
$$450 * (1.12)^{-4} = \$285.98$$
$$450 * (1.12)^{-5} = \$255.34$$
$$5,000 * (1.12)^{-5} = \$2,837.13$$

Total $4,459.28 or $44.59 per share.

Alternatively, noting that the dividends form a stream of payments all of which are the same amount and are equally spaced in time, we could calculate the present value of the ordinary annuity of dividend payments and add the present value of the lump sum payment of $5,000.

Thus:

$450 * (PV annuity factor, n = 5, i = 12%) = $450 * 3.6047 = $1,622.15
$5,000 * (1.12)^{-5}$ = $2,837.13
Total   = $4,459.28

Teaching Notes:

As the first case we use in our course, the Maytag case sets the tone. We have found that using a company well-known to students helps them get off to a good start. The purpose of the case is to become familiar with the contents of a set of financial statements and to begin to think in terms of how economic events are reflected therein.

Some students need to be reminded that the point of the exercise is not to perform a comprehensive analysis of the company. At this point, most students do not have the required skills. Rather, the goal is one of discovery. Many students find that they understand a lot more of the information in the financials than they thought they would. Others find that the vocabulary bogs them down. They need to be encouraged to learn the language of business.

We complement this case with some current business press articles dealing with uses and users of financial information. Building a link from current events to corporate financial reports motivates the user perspective we adopt in the course.

For many students, the most eye-opening part of the case is the last part where they are asked to identify as many of the estimates underlying the financials as they can. Many are surprised to find out that financial statements are not "truth and beauty" but rather are the end result of a series of complex professional judgments. Understanding the role of judgment early on helps students place the rest of the cases in an appropriate perspective.

a. The four commonly prepared financial statements are the balance sheet, the income statement, the cash flow statement and the statement of retained earnings. Maytag uses names that describe the statements; Consolidated Balance Sheets, Consolidated Statements of Income and Consolidated Statements of Cash Flows. The retained earnings statement, not included in the case, is called Consolidated Statements of Shareowners' Equity. Also, beginning in 1998, companies are required to report and display comprehensive income (see "Notes to Consolidated Financial Statements"-"Summary of Significant Accounting Policies"-"Comprehensive Income"). While most companies report comprehensive income as part of one of the four commonly prepared financial statements (for example, in the income statement or statement of retained earnings), Maytag reports comprehensive income in a separate statement, the Consolidated Statements of Comprehensive Income. This statement is not included in the case. "Consolidated" refers to the fact that Maytag's subsidiary companies are included in the financial statements. That is, all the companies owned by Maytag are part of a consolidated group for which one set of financial reports is prepared.

b. Public companies are regulated by the Securities and Exchange Commission. SEC registrants (e.g., Maytag) need to file quarterly financial statements. These are made publicly available. The case includes the annual report, the one prepared at the close of Maytag's fiscal year.

c. There are potentially many users of these financial statements. Users include: current and potential shareowners, current and potential debt investors, competitors, suppliers, customers, government agencies such as the IRS, labor unions, management, employees who contribute to the Maytag pension and accounting students such as yourself.

d. Maytag is in the business of manufacturing home appliances and commercial appliances. We can see from the note "Segment Reporting" that home appliances is the major segment and that most of their sales are in the United States.

e. Maytag is audited by Ernst & Young, LLP, one of the "Big Five" CPA firms. Maytag received an unqualified audit opinion in 1998. An unqualified opinion is the best report a company can receive from its auditors. It means that the auditors have performed their tests and are reasonably sure that the financial statements are free from material misstatement. Note that it *does not* mean that the auditors guarantee that the financial statements are free from all misstatements or that the company is a good investment. They are merely saying that the numbers, as reported, can be relied on.

The first paragraph of the report outlines the scope of the audit. That is, it explains what financial statements and schedules the auditor's opinion covers. The second paragraph outlines, in very general terms, what an audit is. The third paragraph provides the auditor's opinion.

The report is dated February 2, 1999 because that is the date the auditors' field work ended. In other words, the audit took place, in part, during the month after year-end.

f. and **g.** Common-size financial statements - see following pages

MAYTAG CORPORATION
Consolidated Statements of Income
In thousands except per share data

	1998		1997		1996	
			Year ended December 31			
Net sales	4,069,290	100.0%	3,407,911	100.0%	3,001,656	100.0%
Cost of Sales	2,887,663	71.0%	2,471,623	72.5%	2,180,213	72.6%
Gross profit	1,181,627	29.0%	936,288	27.5%	821,443	27.4%
Selling, general and administrative expenses	658,889	16.2%	578,015	17.0%	512,364	17.1%
Restructuring charge					40,000	1.3%
Operating income	522,738	12.8%	358,273	10.5%	269,079	9.0%
Interest expense	(62,765)	-1.5%	(58,995)	-1.7%	(43,006)	-1.4%
Other—net	10,912	0.3%	1,277	0.0%	2,164	0.1%
Income before income taxes, minority interest extraordinary item	470,885	11.6%	300,555	8.8%	228,237	7.6%
Income taxes	176,100	4.3%	109,800	3.2%	89,000	3.0%
Income before minority interest and extraordinary item	294,785	7.2%	190,755	5.6%	139,237	4.6%
Minority interest	(8,275)	-0.2%	(7,265)	-0.2%	(1,260)	0.0%
Income before extraordinary item	286,510	7.0%	183,490	5.4%	137,977	4.6%
Extraordinary item - loss on early retirement of debt	(5,900)	-0.1%	(3,200)	-0.1%	(1,548)	-0.1%
Net income	280,610	6.9%	180,290	5.3%	136,429	4.5%

MAYTAG CORPORATION
Balance Sheets

December 31

Assets	1998		1997	
Current assets				
Cash and cash equivalents	28,642	1.1%	27,991	1.1%
Accounts receivable, net	472,979	18.3%	473,741	18.8%
Inventories	383,753	14.8%	350,209	13.9%
Deferred income taxes	39,014	1.5%	46,073	1.8%
Other current assets	44,474	1.7%	36,703	1.5%
Total current assets	968,862	37.4%	934,717	37.2%
Noncurrent assets				
Deferred income taxes	120,273	4.7%	118,931	4.7%
Prepaid pension cost	1,399	0.1%	2,160	0.1%
Intangible pension asset	62,811	2.4%	33,819	1.4%
Other intangibles, net	424,312	16.4%	433,595	17.3%
Other noncurrent assets	44,412	1.7%	49,660	2.0%
Total noncurrent assets	653,207	25.2%	638,165	25.4%
Property, plant and equipment				
Land	19,317	0.8%	19,597	0.8%
Buildings and improvements	333,032	12.9%	309,960	12.3%
Machinery and equipment	1,499,872	58.0%	1,427,276	56.8%
Construction in progress	102,042	3.9%	59,376	2.4%
Total property, plant and equipment, cost	1,954,263	75.5%	1,816,209	72.2%
Less allowance for depreciation	(988,669)	-38.2%	(874,937)	-34.8%
Total property, plant and equipment, net	965,594	37.3%	941,272	37.4%
Total assets	2,587,663	100.0%	2,514,154	100.0%
Liabilities and Shareowners' Equity				
Current liabilities				
Notes payable	112,898	4.4%	112,843	4.5%
Accounts payable	279,086	10.8%	221,417	8.8%
Compensation to employees	81,836	3.2%	62,758	2.5%
Accrued liabilities	176,701	6.8%	161,344	6.4%
Current maturities of long-term debt	140,176	5.4%	8,276	0.3%
Total current liabilities	790,697	30.6%	566,638	22.5%
Noncurrent liabilities				
Deferred income taxes	21,191	0.8%	23,666	0.9%
Long-term debt, less current portion	446,505	17.3%	549,524	21.9%
Postretirement benefit liability	460,599	17.8%	454,390	18.1%
Accrued pension cost	69,660	2.7%	31,308	1.3%
Other noncurrent liabilities	117,392	4.5%	99,096	3.9%
Total noncurrent liabilities	1,115,347	43.1%	1,157,984	46.1%
Minority interest	174,055	6.7%	173,723	6.9%
Shareowners' equity				
Common stock	146,438	5.7%	146,438	5.8%
Additional paid-in capital	467,192	18.1%	494,646	19.7%
Retained earnings	760,115	29.4%	542,118	21.6%
Cost of common stock in treasury	(805,802)	-31.1%	(508,115)	-20.2%
Employee stock plans	(45,331)	-1.8%	(48,416)	-1.9%
Accumulated other comprehensive income	(15,048)	-0.6%	(10,862)	-0.4%
Total shareowners' equity	507,864	19.6%	615,809	24.5%
Total liabilities and shareowners' equity	2,587,663	100.0%	2,514,154	100.0%

h. i. The asset side of the balance sheet lists the investments made by the company. Property, plant and equipment comprises approximately 37% of total assets in 1998 and 1997 and is the most significant asset on the balance sheet. Other major assets include accounts receivable (1998—18.3%, 1997—18.8%), inventories (1998—14.8%, 1997—13.9%), and intangibles (1998—16.4%, 1994—17.3%).

h. ii. The liability and shareholders' equity side of the balance sheet lists how the assets have been financed. The most significant claims against the company's assets include accounts payable (1998—10.8%, 1997—8.8%), long-term debt (1998—17.3%, 1997—21.9%), postretirement benefit liability (1998—17.8%, 1997—18.1%), and shareowners' equity (1998—19.6%, 1997—24.5%). In later cases, we'll discuss the nuts and bolts of each of these items.

i. i. The common-size income statement reveals that Maytag's revenues are from "Net Sales." The only clues about the company's sources of revenue are included in the "Segment Reporting" footnote. The segment information indicates that home appliances account for approximately 86% ($3,482,842/$4,069,290) of the company's 1998 revenues. The same footnote indicates that approximately 89% ($3,601,790/$4,069,290) of these revenues are generated in the United States. Another 3% of sales are made in the China segment.

i. ii. The common-size income statement provides information about the major categories of expense for the company. Cost of sales has decreased slightly from 72.5% in 1997 to 71.0% in 1998. Costs included in this category are directly attributable to the products that the company sells. Other indirect costs are included in the selling, general and administrative income statement line item. These items amount to 16.2% of 1998 revenues and 17.0% of 1997 revenues. Interest expense has declined from 1.7% of annual revenues in 1997 to only 1.5% in 1998.

i. iii. Over the past three years, net income (or the "bottom line") has increased at Maytag. The company has gone from a profit of $136 million in 1996 to a profit of $281 million in 1998. Note, however, that summary measures of performance — such as Net Income — can be misleading. Indeed, to help investors and creditors make better assessments of a firm's past performance and future prospects, financial statements include detail about the items which comprise summary measures like net income. As you proceed through the cases in this text, you will learn how to evaluate the various line items on the financial statements. You will learn how to subjectively evaluate the "quality" of such line items and their effect on the "persistence" of earnings as you complete subsequent cases.

j. The statement of cash flows provides a general view of where the company's cash came from and went during the year. The statement of cash flows has three sections. The first section, dealing with the cash from Maytag's operations, shows that the company's ongoing operations generated cash of $539,878 during 1998. In fact, Maytag has generated positive operating cash flow for the past three years—a good sign! The investment section follows and reveals that the cash that Maytag received from operations is being used to make capital expenditures (e.g. investments in property, plant, and equipment). Thus, the net cash from investing activities is negative. The last section of the statement, the financing section, shows that dividends, stock repurchases, and debt reduction were significant uses of cash during 1998.

k. i. The footnotes reveal that during 1996 the company announced the restructuring of its major appliance operations. The company consolidated two separate organizational units into a single operation and closed a cooking products plant in Indiana. As a result of these actions, the company recorded a restructuring charge of $40 million (pre-tax) in 1996.

Restructurings of this nature are rare (they do not occur annually), so we would not expect to see an amount in the income statement for restructuring charge for each year presented, as we do with the other line items in the income statement.

To determine whether restructuring charges will recur, we need to determine whether Maytag plans on restructuring operations in the future. Information of this type is found in the Management Discussion and Analysis section of the annual report. Because the company is silent on this issue, we might assume that this charge was one-of-a-kind, not likely to persist.

k. ii. Information is significant (or material) if disclosing it is likely to influence the decisions of financial statement users. As you can imagine, it is a rather elusive concept and is tough to pin down. How do we determine what is material? There are a number of rules of thumb used by auditors, including 5% of net income before taxes, 1% of total assets, and 1% of revenues. For Maytag, these estimates result in materiality thresholds of $22.8 million, $25.9 million, and $40.7 million, respectively.

k. iii. Here are *just a few* of the accounts requiring estimates and professional judgment to determine their balance.

Accounts receivable, less allowance—The allowance for doubtful accounts is an *estimate* of the amounts included in accounts receivable which may not be collected in the future.

Inventories—Inventories are stated at the lower of cost or market (see Maytag's "Notes to Consolidated Financial Statements"). In determining the cost of work-in-process inventories, Maytag *estimates* their stage of completion and assigns costs accordingly. In determining the market value of the inventories the Company *estimates* the amount at which the inventories can be sold. The company also makes estimates as it allocates manufacturing overhead costs to various classes of inventories.

Pension-related asses and accrued pension cost—As described in the "Pension Benefits" notes to the financial statements, this balance is based on *estimates* of appropriate discount rates, future increases in compensation levels, expected long-term rates of return on pension assets, and average remaining service life of employees. Post-retirement benefits other than pensions also require such estimates.

Intangibles—Although a significant amount is amortized over 40 years (see Accounting Policy Note), presumably the remaining intangibles are amortized over the *estimated* period of future benefit. When one company buys the stock of another (at least when it buys the majority of it), an account called 'goodwill' arises. Goodwill represents the difference between the *fair value* of the net identifiable assets acquired and the purchase price of the assets. Thus, the 'goodwill' balance itself is derived from a number of estimates.

Property, Plant and Equipment—As stated in the Significant Accounting Policies note, depreciation is calculated to amortize the cost of the assets over their *estimated* useful lives.

Accrued Liabilities—As indicated in the note to the financial statements, this balance includes a liability for *estimated* costs of honoring product warranties provided to customers.

With the exception of cash, notes payable, accounts payable, income taxes payable, and long-term debt, virtually all accounts making up the financial statements have estimates underlying them.

Teaching Notes:

This case introduces students to the accounting for warranties, a special type of contingency. The discussion of the types of estimates management makes in preparing the financial statements emphasizes, again, that accounting is more of an art than a science.

We integrate income tax accounting issues into the case by asking students to consider the deferred tax implications of the warranty costs. For some students, deferred tax assets arising from warranty costs are more intuitive than deferred tax liabilities which may never be "paid." Maytag's disclosure of the balance sheet location of their deferred tax assets and liabilities is particularly instructive.

Most students find the warranty issues straightforward, but some have trouble (especially with the deferred tax issues). Walking through each entry over the life of the warranty period and showing how, in the end, the cash flows and the expenses are equal helps these students understand the relationships.

Maytag Corporation—Warranties & Deferred Taxes

a. From a consumer's point of view, a warranty is a performance guarantee. The seller of a good promises to rectify any product deficiencies and spells out the details of this promise in a warranty. Guarantees on a product's performance often increase sales.

b. From an accrual accounting perspective, a warranty is a contingent liability (or loss). The seller of a good under warranty can expect to pay warranty related costs at some point in the future. A promise to pay in the future (as a result of a past event) is the definition of a liability under accrual accounting. Because the sale of the product creates this liability, the future costs associated with the warranty claims are matched to the sale and recorded in the same period.

c. Several judgments need to be made in order to account for warranty costs. Consider the washing machines sold by Maytag. Maytag needs to estimate how many machines will require servicing, of those, how many will actually be serviced (i.e., how many customers will remember that the machine is under warranty and get it fixed by an authorized serviceperson), and what the projected cost per repair will be. For Maytag, this may not be too hard. They have been in the business for many years. However, if a product is significantly different than others they make, their past experience may not be a good guide. In that case, they would be unlikely to ignore the warranty accrual (their auditors would not likely let that get by) but the accrual may not be very precise. As they gain experience with the product, they would adjust the liability to reflect that new knowledge.

d. Because warranty expenses are deducted from book income in the period they are incurred (normally, the period of the sale) but are deducted for tax purposes only when they are paid (normally, in a period later than the sale), a deferred tax asset arises. That is, the company has future tax deductions available to it. The value of those deductions is the amount of the deduction times the expected future tax rate. This implicitly assumes the company will have future taxable income and ignores present value considerations.

e. i.

Dr.	Accounts receivable	175,000,000
Cr.	Sales		175,000,000

(500,000 x $350)
To record sales of 500,000 units during the year.

Dr.	COGS	100,000,000
Cr.	Inventory		100,000,000

(500,000 x $200)
To record the cost of 500,000 units sold during the year.

Dr.	Warranty Expense	2,500,000
Cr.	Accrued Warranty Liability		2,500,000

(500,000 x 5% x $100)
To accrue expected warranty expenses on 500,000 units sold during the year.

e. ii.

Dr.	Accrued Warranty Liability	1,200,000
Cr.	Cash		1,200,000

(12,000 x $100)
To record warranty costs paid during 2000.

e. iii.

```
2001
Dr.    Accrued Warranty Liability                       600,000
Cr.          Cash                                                    600,000
       (6,000 x $100)
To record warranty costs paid during 2001.


2002
Dr.    Accrued Warranty Liability                       700,000
Dr.    Warranty Expense                                  50,000
Cr.          Cash                                                    750,000
       (7,500 x $100)
To record warranty costs paid during 2002.
```

f. At the beginning of 2000, there was neither a book nor a tax balance for the warranty deductions—the sales had not yet taken place. By the end of 2000, the company had booked all $2,500,000 of warranty expense for book purposes, but only the $1,200,000 it paid for tax purposes. Consequently at the end of 2000, Maytag had recorded a liability for accounting purposes of $1,300,000 but a liability of $0 for tax purposes. Because the warranty liability for accounting purposes was $1,300,000 greater than it was for tax purposes, Maytag had a deferred tax asset of [(1,300,000 - 0) * 36% =] $468,000. That is, it had $1,300,000 of future tax deductions at 36%. The following journal entry would be booked in 2000 (see the T-account that follows):

```
Dr.    Deferred Tax Asset (B/S)                        468,000
Cr.          Deferred Tax Expense (I/S)                               468,000
To adjust the DTA and record income tax expense arising from warranty cost.
```

Note that the credit to Deferred Income Tax Expense serves to reduce total income tax expense for book purposes. Income Tax Expense is made up of:

Current Tax Expense (Taxable income * tax rate)
plus Debits to Deferred Tax Expense
less Credits to Deferred Tax Expense.

For 2001, Maytag paid another $600,000 for warranties. These were tax deductible. At the end of 2001, the future deductible amounts for warranties were ($2,500,000 - 1,200,000 - 600,000) = $700,000 (i.e., the balance in the Accrued Warranty Liability account). At a tax rate of 36%, that leaves a deferred tax asset of $252,000 at the end of 2001. The journal entry to record the change in the Deferred Tax Asset account is:

```
Dr.    Deferred Tax Expense (I/S)                      216,000
Cr.          Deferred Tax Asset (B/S)                                 216,000
To adjust the DTA and record income tax expense arising from warranty cost.
```

Note that the debit to Deferred Tax Expense increases the book tax expense; (other things equal, it is higher than current taxes payable). This makes sense. After all, in the first year, taxes payable were higher than tax expense (remember, we deducted an amount from overall tax expense when we set up the deferred tax asset), this year as the tax deductions become available, the difference reverses.

Finally, the remainder of the deferred tax asset reverses when the 2002 warranty payments are made. By the end of 2002, there is no future deductible amount for tax purposes and thus the deferred tax asset balance should be *zero* (i.e., both the accounting liability and the tax liability for warranties is zero). To arrive at that balance we book the following entry:

```
Dr.    Deferred Tax Expense (I/S)                        252,000
Cr.            Deferred Tax Asset (B/S)                            252,000
```
To adjust the DTA and record income tax expense arising from warranty cost.

Deferred Tax Asset

1/1/00	0		
set up asset	468,000		
12/31/00	468,000		
		216,000	reverse difference
12/31/01	252,000		
		252,000	reverse difference
12/31/02	0		

g. i.

Warranties (B/S)

		37,732,000	12/31/97
Payments	40,000,000	48,430,000	Expense (plug)
		46,162,000	12/31/98

g. ii.
```
Dr.    Warranty Expense                               48,430,000
Cr.            Warranties (B/S)                                 48,430,000
```
To accrue warranty expenses for 1998.

```
Dr.    Warranties (B/S)                               40,000,000
Cr.            Cash                                            40,000,000
```
To record warranty costs paid during 1998.

h.   The warranty accrual (B/S) account increased because more warranty costs were newly incurred (expensed for accounting purposes) than were paid (and thus tax deductible). If Maytag recorded greater warranty expenses for accounting purposes than for tax purposes, future deductible amounts for tax (over and above the deduction available for accounting) increased. This implies that the deferred tax asset related to warranties should increase over the year.

i.   The deferred tax asset for warranties/liabilities increased during the year. However, the increase in the deferred tax asset of $6,377,000 is 75.6% of the increase in the warranty accrual, which is higher than the typical 30-40% relationship (the deferred tax asset should approximately reflect the tax rate applied to the temporary difference between book carrying amount and tax basis). It appears that Maytag has aggregated deferred tax assets related to other types of liability with the warranty tax asset. Alternatively, the tax rate related to the book-tax difference in the warranty liability may have increased in 1998 (more than offsetting the decrease in the book-tax difference). Finally, there may be long-term warranty liabilities which are not included in the "accrued liabilities" category of the B/S. These, too, would give rise to DTAs, but were not considered in our analysis. All three reasons might explain the apparent conflict.

This is a good example of using information from different parts of the financial statements to understand a particular item. An analyst faced with this or other conflicting information could call the investor relations department for further clarification.

Teaching notes:

This case requires students to think backwards. Backing the R&D expense out of net income and working with the incremental effect of the capitalization is challenging and some students may choose to re-cast the entire income statement. The effects of income taxes may be ignored by some students and some may discuss deferred taxes.

The case points out that different accounting rules will yield different financials despite the fact that the economics of the situation are the same. A discussion of the potential consequences of the capitalization decision (such as reactions by financial statement users) can follow up on the income statement numbers.

Although the question does not require a comparison of the two net income figures and the three balance sheets, a discussion of the differences is instructive. Point out that income is higher under capitalization only when R&D expenditures are growing.

The fact that cash is not affected will not surprise many students but the changes in the cash flow statement will stump some.

a.   Likely types of costs include:

- wages, benefits, pensions and other employment related expenses for the 8,500 R & D personnel
- supplies necessary to conduct research
- research facilities and equipment which would be capitalized as fixed assets and charged to R & D as depreciation
- legal costs associated with patent applications
- overhead charges for personnel related indirectly to R & D
- research related travel, conference fees, costs to host conferences
- cost of academic publications subscribed to by R & D personnel

b.   The CICA principles provide a better matching of costs and benefits because deferred development costs will be amortized when commercial production starts (and revenues are being earned). This is especially critical for a pharmaceutical developer like Merck because sales revenue follows development by several years while regulatory approval is sought.

However, an associated drawback is that there is some uncertainty related to recoverability of deferred development costs. In the case of Merck, this drawback is mitigated somewhat by the existence of patents which limit entry by a competitor and thus assure (to some extent) the recoverability of the development costs. However, determining whether a drug will recover its development costs is inherently judgmental.

c. i.

Total R & D 1989 to 1998 (from Form 10-K)	$ 12,000.0
1994 expenses (given in the question)	1,230.6
1995 expenses (given in the question)	1,331.4
1996 expenses (from the Income Stmt)	1,487.3
1997 expenses (from the Income Stmt)	1,683.7
1998 expenses (from the Income Stmt)	<u>1,821.1</u>
Pre-1994 (1989 to 1993 inclusive)	$ <u>4,445.9</u>

c. ii.

Dr.	Research and Development Expense	1,821.1
Cr.	Wages and Benefits Payable	
Cr.	Supplies Inventory	
Cr.	Accumulated Depreciation	
Cr.	Legal Fees Payable	
Cr.	Other Payables	
Cr.	Cash	
	Total:	1,821.1

To record R&D costs for 1998

d. i.

	1998	1997	1996
Income Before Taxes	$8,133.1	$6,462.3	$5,540.8
add: 25% of R & D	455.3	420.9	371.8
Less: amortization of deferred development (1994)			153.8
Less: amortization of deferred development (1995)		166.4	166.4
Less: amortization of deferred development (1996)	185.9	185.9	
Less: amortization of deferred development (1997)	210.5		
Adjusted Income Before Tax	8,192.0	6,530.9	5,592.4
Taxes on Income	2,905.8	1,867.8	1,675.0
Income before cumulative effect of accounting changes	$5,286.2	$4,663.1	$3,917.4

d. ii.

Year	Annual R & D	25% Development	Cumulative Development	Unamortized Portion *	Accumulated Amortization (plug)
Pre-1994	4,445.9	1,111.5	1,111.5	–	–
1994	1,230.6	307.7	1,419.2	–	–
1995	1,331.4	332.9	1,752.1	–	–
1996	1,487.3	371.8	2,123.9	538.3	1,585.6
1997	1,683.7	420.9	2,544.8	606.8	1,938.0
1998	1,821.1	455.3	3,000.0	665.8	2,334.2
Total from Form 10-K	12,000.0	–	–	–	–

* Unamortized portion is the current year's capitalized amount plus one half of the prior year's capitalized amount.
1996:   371.8 + .5(332.9) = 538.3
1997:   420.9 + .5(371.8) = 606.8
1998:   455.3 + .5(420.9) = 665.8

d. iii.   Assuming that the tax treatment of R&D remains unchanged, there is no change in Merck's cash inflows or outflows for the year because of the capitalization of development costs. The year-end cash balances remain unchanged.

The Statement of Cash Flows will be affected. Because net income is changed by the capitalization of the development costs, the opening number on the cash flow statement will be different. The amortization of development costs (a non-cash expense) will be added back in the operations section. As well, the investment section will reflect the additional capitalized amount for the year.

d. iv.   The conservative nature of U.S. GAAP for R&D means that the balance sheet does not capture the expected future benefits of R&D expenditures. This is a result of placing a premium on reliability and verifiability over relevance. Managers need to find means other than the financial statements to communicate the success of their R&D efforts.

However, as we saw with Merck, the income statement is not as severely affected as the balance sheet. Indeed, should economic assets related to the R&D exist, they ought to show up on the I/S in increased profitability. For a company like Merck that has both a steady stream of R&D expenditures and a steady stream of new drugs, the income statement effect of U.S. R&D accounting is minor. For new firms or firms with growing R&D expenditures, the I/S is likely to understate profitability. On the other hand the Balance Sheet will be missing an important asset and thus will not provide a complete representation of the company's economic position.

As noted in part 1., total cash flows are unaffected. However, capitalized R&D shows up in the investing section of the SCF and expensed R&D shows up in the operating section.

In summary, the main weaknesses of U.S. GAAP for R&D are: understating B/S assets and delaying the recognition of profitability for new firms or growing firms that have successful R&D efforts.

Analysts wishing to compensate for these weaknesses should carefully read other disclosures about R&D performance in the Form 10-K and review patent filing and trade publications.

Nike—Basic Ratio Analysis

Teaching Notes:

This case in basic ratio analysis helps students see how financial statements can be *used* early in the course. We do not believe that financial statement analysis should be left to the end (time permitting) of a course in financial accounting. We introduce basic tools early on and add more sophisticated ones as we look at specific accounts (e.g., accounts receivable turnover when we discuss receivables).

Although most students like the user approach, a small minority become frustrated because they are still struggling with basic terminology issues. We win them over by making sure they understand that cases like Nike and Maytag are designed to familiarize students with financial accounting and that we do not expect them to be able to see all the subtleties at this early stage.

Nike—Basic Ratio Analysis

a. Solvency measures such as the current ratio and working capital, represent the firm's ability to meet its current obligations using current assets.

Return on Assets (ROA) and Return on Equity (ROE) are measures of earning power or profitability. Return on equity measures the income of the firm relative to the owners' investment. Return on assets measures the income of the firm relative to the resources available to produce income.

Ratio analysis is an important way to assess the solvency and earnings power of a company. Financial ratios are frequently used in contracting with the firm by outside parties such as investors (e.g., in management compensation contracts) and creditors (e.g., through restrictive debt covenants). The ratios illustrated in this case are only a few of the many frequently used by investors, creditors, and financial analysts.

b.

Ratio	1995 Computation	1995	1994
i. current ratio	2,045,928 / 1,107,535	1.85	3.15
ii. working capital	2,045,928 - 1,107,535	938,393	1,208,444
iii. Gross margin percent	((4,760,834 - 2,865,280) / 4,760,834) * 100	39.8%	39.3%
iv. return on equity (ROE)	399,664 / [(1,964,689 + 1,740,949) / 2]	0.216	0.177
v. return on assets (ROA)	[399,664 + 24,208 (1 - .385)] / [(3,142,745 + 2,373,815) / 2]	0.150	0.135

Note: some texts calculate ROA as net income divided by average total assets. We add interest expense back to net income when we calculate ROA because the measure then reflects the return on assets earned by managers without concern for how the assets were financed. This makes particular sense if the measure is used to evaluate the performance of managers who do not control financing decisions or to compare the performance of two companies that finance their investments with different levels of debt. A more precise measure of ROA adds back interest expense net of tax (i.e., interest expense (1 - tax rate)). This takes into account the tax savings provided by interest expense. Without interest expense, pretax income would be higher and so income tax expense would be higher.

The preceding discussion illustrates an important point: ratios are not set in stone. Different analysts (and textbook authors) calculate them in different ways. You should keep this in mind whenever you compare "precomputed" ratios, especially across companies.

c. Net income increased by $100,870,000 (33.8%) during fiscal year 1995. The major reason is the increase in sales (about $971 million) from higher volume and higher prices. Nike's gross margin percent also increased to 39.8% (up 0.5% from 1994). Although selling and administrative expenses were up $236 million, as an overall percentage of sales, S&A expenses decreased from the prior year (25.4% vs. 25.7%), indicating they were relatively constant compared to sales volume.

d. One way to measure profitability is to deflate income by shareholders' equity or total assets so that a common measure can be compared across firms or periods. Because companies with more capital should earn more income, dividing net income by the capital base is a useful measure. Return on equity rose from 0.177 in 1994 to 0.216 in 1995, a 22% increase. Return on assets increased from 0.135 in 1994 to 0.150 in 1995, a 12% increase. By these measures, Nike was more profitable in 1995.

Note that we did not adjust the ROE ratio for the preferred dividends. This was because the financial statements did not provide the split between the common and preferred dividends.

e. $216,071

f. The current ratio of 1.85 and positive working capital of $938,393 indicate that Nike *was* in a position to pay its short-term obligations at May 31, 1995. That is, they had $1.85 of highly liquid assets for every dollar of debt due in the next year. A more stringent test of solvency is the quick ratio ([cash + marketable securities + accounts receivable] / current liabilities). This ratio was 1.15 at May 31, 1995. As many companies have a quick ratio below 1.0, Nike, Inc. is in a relatively good position to pay off its immediate obligations.

g. The statement of cash flows indicates that operations provided $254,913 of cash during the fiscal year ended May 31, 1995. Note that although net income increased by about 25% between 1994 and 1995, cash flow from operations decreased by 56%, mainly due to the large increase in accounts receivable.

Note: the relatively large increase in accounts receivable (50%) compared to the increase in sales (26%) should raise some questions. Did Nike record large sales at year end to boost 1995 profit? Did the company engage in aggressive revenue recognition—thus lowering the "quality" of 1995 earnings? We return to these issues in later cases.

h. The main source of cash was operations ($254,913) and issuances of notes payable ($263,874). Significant uses of cash include acquisitions of property, plant and equipment ($154,125), the acquisition of new subsidiaries, including Canstar Sports Inc.—the world's largest hockey equipment manufacturer ($430,020), the repurchase of Nike stock ($142,919), the reduction of long term debt ($39,804), and preferred and common dividends paid ($65,418).

Teaching Notes:

In this case, students learn the concept of deferred taxes. The case analyzes SFAS 109 disclosures made by the Robert Mondavi Corporation. The first few questions explore why accountants record deferred tax expenses and what deferred tax assets and liabilities represent.

The case goes on to analyze two components of Mondavi's net deferred tax liability. The first, PP&E, is the largest element. After describing the reason for the liability, students are asked to use the note disclosure to infer the tax balance for property, plant and equipment. This is a particularly useful analytical tool because sometimes the tax treatment of an item is close to an alternative accounting treatment for the item. By estimating the tax balance, users can adjust the balance for financial reporting to the alternative method if desired.

The second analysis combines deferred tax accounting with revenue recognition issues. Students read Mondavi's wine futures program footnote and determine the accounting treatment of receipts under the program. Armed with that information and an assumption about the tax treatment of the receipts, they determine how deferred taxes are affected.

Overall, this case proves to be very challenging even for good students. We have included elements in each part that all students should be able to handle.

The Robert Mondavi Corporation—Deferred Taxes

a. The objective of deferred tax accounting under SFAS 109 is the recognition of the tax consequences of a transaction or an event in the same period that the transaction or event is recognized in the company's *financial statements* (Deloitte & Touche: Accounting for income taxes, 1992). The Robert Mondavi Corporation reports deferred income taxes as part of its total income tax expense because, for financial reporting purposes, tax expense is based on the *financial reporting* values of assets and liabilities. If revenue is (is not) recognized in the financial statements then there should be, other things equal, more (less) tax expense for financial reporting purposes regardless of how the revenue is treated for tax purposes. If an expense is (is not) recognized for accounting purposes, then, other things equal, there should be less (more) income tax expense reported on the income statement, regardless of how the expense is treated for tax purposes. An important exception to both these examples is when the revenue or expense will never be recognized for tax purposes. Those differences are referred to as permanent differences.

An important reason for coming up with a different measure of tax expense lies in the different goals of financial reporting and the tax system. Financial reporting is driven by a desire to match costs and benefits. The tax system is not driven by such a goal. Often, tax laws are created to stimulate a particular industry or to encourage or discourage a particular behavior. For example, allowing accelerated depreciation for tax purposes makes fixed assets cheaper than if the straight-line basis was prescribed for tax purposes. Getting the tax deductions sooner doesn't change the total tax paid over the life of the asset but it does reduce the present value of those taxes. For reporting purposes however, we'd like to match the cost of the asset with the benefits it produces and we may decide that straight-line depreciation does a better job than accelerated depreciation.

Consequently, we base tax expense on financial reporting-based asset and liability measurement (and ultimately accounting income), while taxes payable are based on tax-based asset and liability measurement (and ultimately taxable income). Reporting income tax expense as equal to the current tax bill ignores the future tax benefits and costs that are not reflected in accounting income.

For example, assume Robert Mondavi has a level stream of revenues and expenses (other than depreciation) for the next ten years. In the first year, the Company buys some new equipment. Suppose Mondavi immediately writes the equipment off for tax purposes, but, for accounting purposes, depreciates it over ten years. Using the current tax bill as accounting tax expense would yield relatively little tax expense in the first year because the full tax deduction was taken that year. In future years, there would be higher tax expense because no tax deduction is left. However, other things equal, income *before* tax for accounting purposes would be the same each year. Using the tax bill as tax expense would lead to changing *net* income over time even though nothing was different economically. Deferred tax accounting avoids this problem.

Continuing the Mondavi equipment example, under deferred tax accounting, in the first year, we would have a higher accounting tax expense than the current tax bill because accounting depreciation would be less than the tax deduction. We would set up a deferred tax liability for the difference between taxes payable and the expense. The journal entry would be:

```
Dr.    Income Tax Expense                              xxx
Cr.        Taxes Payable                                       xxx
Cr.        Deferred Tax Liability                              xxx
```

In future years, the current tax bill would be greater than the accounting expense because the accounting depreciation would be greater than the tax deduction. The journal entry in those years would be:

```
Dr.    Income Tax Expense                              xxx
Dr.    Deferred Tax Liability                          xxx
Cr.        Taxes Payable                                       xxx
```

Over time, the deferred tax liability reverses (goes to zero), the income statements show tax expense at the same level each year, and the balance sheets reflect the deferred tax liabilities that exist because future years will not have the depreciation deductions available for tax purposes that will be recorded for accounting purposes.

b.   Deferred tax assets arise when the book value of an asset is less than the tax basis asset value or when the book value of a liability is greater than the tax basis liability value.

This happens when a company records revenue or gains for tax purposes prior to recording them for accounting purposes (or expenses or losses are recorded for tax purposes after they are recorded for accounting purposes).

An example is post-retirement benefits other than pensions. These costs are recorded for accounting purposes before they are deducted for tax purposes. That means that the accounting liability for post-retirement benefits is greater than the tax basis liability. When the cash payments are made, they will not affect net income (they've already been recorded as expenses) but they will be deductible for tax purposes. Consequently, the accounting liability is related to a future tax deduction. That future tax deduction is a deferred tax asset.

Deferred tax liabilities arise when the book value of an asset is more than the tax basis asset value or when the book value of a liability is less than the tax basis liability value.

This happens when a company records revenue or gains for tax purposes after recording them for accounting purposes (or expenses or losses are recorded for tax purposes before they are recorded for accounting purposes).

An example is the use of accelerated depreciation for tax purposes and straight-line for reporting purposes. Initially, the net book value of PP&E is greater for accounting than for tax. When accounting depreciation is taken it will be less than the tax deduction. Consequently, there is a tax liability associated with the net book value of the PP&E: in future years accounting depreciation will be greater than tax depreciation. That liability is a deferred tax liability.

c.   The deferred tax liability of $8,374 is made up of Deferred income taxes of $570 (in current assets) and Deferred income taxes of $8,944 (in long-term liabilities).

d.
```
Dr.    Income tax expense                          16,029
Dr.    Deferred tax assets                            227
Dr.    Deferred tax liabilities                       262
Cr.        Taxes payable                                    16,518
```
To record 1996 income tax expense.

The figures in this journal entry are derived as follows. Income tax expense is from the income statement and agrees with the first table in note 8. Taxes payable is the sum of the Current Federal and State taxes as disclosed in the first table in note 8. The debits to the deferred tax assets and liabilities accounts are derived as the changes in the Gross Deferred Tax Assets and Gross Deferred Tax Liabilities disclosed in the third table of note 8. The current deferred tax assets and liabilities are netted and disclosed on the balance sheet, as are the non-current deferred tax assets and liabilities.

e. i. The deferred tax liability arose because Mondavi wrote off its property, plant and equipment faster for tax than for accounting. Thus, the book value of the net PP&E is greater than the tax value of the asset.

e. ii. The deferred tax liability for the property, plant and equipment is $11,431. It represents the difference in tax basis and book value of net PP&E times the tax rate (assumed to be the effective tax rate reported in 1996 of 39.6%). Thus, the difference is $28,866. The book value for tax purposes of the PP&E is, therefore, $127,888. ($156,754 - $28,866)

f. i. Under a wine futures program distributors buy wine from the company before it is ready for sale in the hope that its value will rise (allowing them to sell at the higher price) or ensuring that they will be able to procure relatively rare wines.

From Mondavi's point of view, it has received deferred revenue. When it gets the cash it records:

```
Dr.   Cash                                          xxx
Cr.          Deferred Revenue                              xxx
```

When the wine is delivered, it records:

```
Dr.   Deferred Revenue                              xxx
Cr.          Revenue                                       xxx
```

f. ii. If the receipts were considered income for tax purposes but not for accounting purposes, then there would be a deferred tax asset for accounting purposes. That is, the book value of the deferred revenue liability is greater than its tax value.

f. iii. Note 1 indicates that deferred revenue related to the wine futures program shows up in two places on the balance sheet: the Deferred revenue account (current liabilities) and also as a portion of the Other liabilities account (long term liabilities). Together, the total deferred revenue balances have increased in fiscal 1996 [(1,682 + 23 =) 1,705 vs. 1,507 (= 1,493 + 14)].

For tax purposes, Mondavi's wine futures program has a liability (deferred revenue) of $0. That is, they have recorded the cash inflows as revenues already. Consequently, because the difference between the book value and the tax value of the liability increased, so did the deferred tax asset associated with the difference.

We can estimate the increase in the deferred tax asset as the change in the book-tax difference ([$1,705 - 0] - [$1,507 - 0] = 198) times the tax rate (39.6% in 1996) or $78.

The Seagram Company—Investments in Common Stock

Teaching Notes:

This case contrasts the accounting treatment of intercorporate investments. Seagram has three high-profile investments, each accounted for differently.

Their investment in Time Warner is less than 20% and accordingly, is accounted for at market value. Interesting class discussion can be generated by asking why Seagram would invest in a media company (the article, The Mogul, sheds some light). In addition, discussion of Time Warner's poison pill defense to avoid takeover by Seagram makes for a lively class session (and helps explain why Seagram has not accumulated more Time Warner stock).

Seagram's investment in DuPont is accounted for using the equity method, because they own approximately 24% of the DuPont stock. Seagram discloses this investment in a unique fashion—one that confuses some students. On the income statement, Seagram separately discloses the dividends it receives from DuPont and the "unremitted equity" in DuPont earnings. Together, the two amounts add to equal Seagram's share of DuPont's earnings, however their disclosure highlights the important cash flow impact of the investment.

Finally, Seagram recently announced that it was selling its investment in DuPont back to the company. Seagram also announced that it would use a part of the proceeds to purchase a majority interest in MCA. Discussing reasons why DuPont would buy back the stock (rather than allow Seagram to sell the shares on the open market) helps students understand the impact on market price (and potential takeovers) of selling large blocks of shares. The MCA acquisition incorporates some basic consolidation issues.

Overall, the case provides a good overview of different methods of accounting for intercorporate investments and also allows for class discussion of a number of issues in corporate strategy.

a. January 31, 1995 investment in Time Warner equals $2,043 million. January 31, 1994 investment in Time Warner equals $1,769.

b. January 31, 1995 investment in DuPont equals $3,670 million. January 31, 1994 investment in DuPont equals $3,154 million.

c. Seagram uses the *equity method* to account for its investment in DuPont. Accounting standards prescribe use of the equity method when an investor has "significant influence" in an investee—regardless of the ownership percentage. Guidelines suggest that an investor company should use the equity method when it owns between 20 and 50 percent of the voting shares of an investee. In the case of Seagram's investment in DuPont, significant influence appears to exist. First, Note 1 indicates that Seagram is guaranteed representation on DuPont's Board of Directors in direct proportion to its ownership interest. Second, Seagram is the largest single holder of DuPont shares. By controlling a large block of shares, the Seagram can exert significant influence over DuPont's operations.

d. The Time Warner investment is accounted for under the *market value* approach prescribed by *SFAS No. 115*. Therefore, the account is not adjusted for the income activity of the investee. The FASB prescribes this type of accounting when an investor cannot exert significant influence in an investee. As such, the investment is accounted for in a more "passive" manner.

e. For each dollar of Time Warner's dividends, Seagram would recognize its proportionate share on the income statement (i.e., $0.149). The journal entry for $1 of Time Warner's dividends is:

Dr.	Cash	0.149	
Cr.	Dividend income		0.149

To record cash dividends received.

This accounting reflects the passive nature of Seagram's relationship with Time Warner. Because Seagram cannot exert significant influence, it cannot affect income or dividend policy. Interestingly, this type of accounting seems appropriate for the investment in Time Warner considering the existence of a "poison pill" defense against any single investor owning more than 15% of Time Warner's stock (this poison pill has proved to be controversial and likely explains why Seagram has not increased its investment in Time Warner.)

f. For each share of Time Warner that Seagram owns, it would record a $1 increase in its investment account and a $1 increase in the OE account "Cumulative gain on equity securities." As Seagram owns 56.8 million shares of time Warner, the entry would be:

Dr.	Common Stock of Time Warner, Inc., at market value	56,800,000	
Cr.	Cumulative gain on equity securities (OE)		56,800,000

To adjust Time Warner stock to market value.

This type of market value adjustment is designed to reflect the "real" value of Seagram's assets. This type of accounting is preferred to historical-cost accounting for investments because it more clearly reflects the financial strength (or weakness) of a company that has extensive equity holdings. Because the Time Warner shares are considered 'available for sale,' the unrealized gain or loss is booked to owners' equity and not the income statement. When the shares are sold the cumulative gain or loss will appear on the income statement.

g. For each dollar of DuPont's net income, Seagram would recognize income in proportion to its ownership interest DuPont's voting shares (i.e., $0.241). The journal entry for $1 of DuPont's income is:

```
Dr.   Common Stock of E.I. DuPont de Nemours, at equity        0.241
Cr.          Equity in unremitted DuPont earnings (I/S)                    0.241
To record share of DuPont earnings.
```

Because Seagram can exert significant influence in DuPont's operating and investment activities, accounting standards place "substance over form" and reduce the barriers between the two entities. Therefore, the equity method provides accounting information "as if" DuPont was a partially owned subsidiary of Seagram.

h.   For each dollar of DuPont's dividends, Seagram would reduce its DuPont investment account by a proportionate share (i.e., $0.241). The journal entry for $1 of DuPont's dividends is as follows:

```
Dr.   Cash                                                     0.241
Cr.          Common Stock of E.I. DuPont de Nemours, at equity           0.241
To record cash dividends received.
```

The DuPont investment account is reduced because dividends represent the distribution of previously accumulated earnings. Because Seagram exerts significant influence, it can also influence the declaration of dividends. Income is recognized during the earnings process and dividends are payments of the earnings accumulated during that process.

i.   There is no journal entry for stock price movements under the equity method. The primary reason is that DuPont is accounted for "as if" it were proportionately part of the Seagram organization. Companies do not recognize gains and losses from the price movements of their own stock. In addition, as a practical matter, market value accounting is supposed to approximate what a company could get for its stake in an investee if it was liquidated. If Seagram's entire block of DuPont shares were released on the open market, the excess supply likely would significantly depress the price of DuPont's stock. (As you will see in a later part of this case, a direct buy-back by DuPont can mitigate this potential problem.)

j.   Not exactly. First, DuPont's reporting period is a calendar year and Seagram's is a fiscal year ending January 31. The financial accounting information presented in Note 1 is based on DuPont's calendar-based reporting year while the proportionate share of DuPont's income recognized in Seagram's financial statements is from the year ending January 1 (i.e., eleven months from DuPont's December 31, 1994 net income disclosed in Note 1 and the first month from year ending December 31, 1995 that is not disclosed). In Note 1, DuPont's balance sheet information is based on DuPont's historical costs. However, the DuPont investment account carried on Seagram's books is based on the market price of their initial investment in DuPont's stock, adjusted for their proportionate share of DuPont's income and dividends since acquisition.

k.   Seagram will receive $8.8 billion for its stake in DuPont. The hypothetical journal entry is:

```
Dr.   Cash                                                     8,800
Cr.          Common Stock of E.I. DuPont de Nemours at equity            3,670
Cr.          Gain on sale of DuPont (pre-tax)                            5,130
To record sale of DuPont.
```

1.

	(Column 1) Information from Seagram's 1995 Balance Sheet	(Column 2) Proposed Sale of DuPont Common Stock	(Column 3) Pro-forma Balance Sheet (after DuPont Sale)	(Column 4) Purchase of 80% of MCA Common Stock	(Column 5) Pro-forma Balance Sheet (after DuPont Sale and MCA purchase)	(Column 6) Consolidating (ledger) Journal Entry	(Column 7) Pro-forma Consolidated Balance Sheet (after DuPont Sale and MCA purchase)
Current assets	4,176	8,800	12,976	(5,700)	7,276	2,500	9,776
Excess of cost over fair value of assets acquired	1,547	-	1,547	-	1,547	500	2,047
Other noncurrent assets	7,233	(3,670)	3,563	5,700	9,263	9,000 (5,700)	12,563
Current liabilities	4,091	-	4,091	-	4,091	2,000	6,091
Noncurrent liabilities	3,356	-	3,356	-	3,356	3,000 1,300	7,656
Shareholders' equity	5,509	5,130	10,639	-	10,639	-	10,639

m. Seagram proposed to purchase 80% of MCA's outstanding common stock for $5.7 billion. The total fair market value of MCA is estimated at $7.125 billion ($5.7 / .8 = $7.125).

n. Seagram's hypothetical journal entry for the proposed purchase of 80% of MCA's outstanding common stock is:

Dr.   Common Stock of MCA, Inc., at equity   5,700
Cr.   Cash   5,700
To record purchase of MCA stock.

Seagram would use the *equity method* to account for its investment in MCA. However, the 80% share of the market values of the assets and liabilities of MCA, Inc. would be consolidated into Seagram's balances for financial reporting purposes. This basis of presentation is referred to as a *consolidation.*

o. See worksheet.

p. See worksheet.

Teaching Notes:

GAAP for marketable securities falls under SFAS No. 115 which was required for fiscal years beginning after December 15, 1993. The approach taken involves an assessment of the corporation's intent (whether they will hold or trade the securities) and an estimation of their market value. These two issues can lead to a lively discussion of how to measure intent, the opportunity for management's manipulation of accounting numbers and of whether market values for securities fit in among the other assets and liabilities recorded at historical cost.

SFAS No. 115 takes a balance sheet perspective. Some marketable securities are marked to market, some are not. The income statement does not reflect, in full, all the market value adjustments. Students are quick to point out these discrepancies and a discussion surrounding the trade-off of the balance sheet vs. the income statement can be started.

An interesting bit of history is that during 1995, FASB issued "A Guide to Implementation of Statement 115 on Accounting for Certain Investments in Debt and Equity Securities." This cleared up some unresolved issues concerning "intent" and caused many firms to reclassify their portfolios.

Beginning in 1998, firms must report Other Comprehensive Income (SFAS No. 130) in the shareholders' equity section of the balance sheet and provide a reconciliation of activity in the account during the year in the statement of shareholders' equity. Unrealized gains and losses on securities available for sale are held in the other comprehensive income account. The reconciliation, included with the case, creates the opportunity to explore this relatively new standard and discuss the implications of market value accounting in general.

Wachovia Corporation—Marketable Securities

a. i. Debt and equity securities classified as "trading" are securities that the company expects to trade in the ordinary course of business. Some balance sheets show "trading liabilities"- these are short trading positions. Both trading assets and liabilities are carried at market value on the balance sheet. That is, they are "marked to market" at the end of the reporting period. The unrealized gains or losses that arise when the trading assets are marked to market are recorded in income for the current period.

a. ii. Debt and equity securities classified as "available-for-sale" are securities that the company may sell in the coming period. Often these securities are held to meet liquidity needs as they arise. These securities are marked to market and carried at market value on the balance sheet. While the asset is adjusted to reflect unrealized gains and losses there is NO income statement effect as for trading assets. Unrealized gains and losses on available for sale securities do not have an income statement effect until the security is actually sold and the gain or loss is realized. Rather, these unrealized gains and or losses, net of any related deferred taxes, are recorded in a separate shareholders' equity account called, for example, net unrealized gains on securities. On the balance sheet this account is often included in the "accumulated other comprehensive income" account.

a. iii. Debt securities that a company intends to hold until they mature may be classified as held-to-maturity. These securities are reported at amortized cost on the balance sheet. Amortized cost represents the cost of the security. Any discount or premium associated with the security is amortized over the time remaining to maturity. The important distinction is that held to maturity securities are NOT marked to market. The rationale for this treatment is that if a company does not intend to sell the security, its market value is considered irrelevant. Therefore, unrealized gains or losses on held-to-maturity securities are not recorded in the financial statements in any way. However, firms must disclose in footnotes to the financial statements, the fair-market value of these securities to comply with SFAS No. 107.

Equity securities cannot be classified as held-to-maturity because they have no fixed maturity date like debt securities do (e.g. bonds and T-bills).

b. i. Wachovia Corp. has trading account assets. Footnote A says that these are derivative and non-derivative financial instruments. The company holds these in anticipation of market movements.

b. ii. The 1999 balance sheet reports $870,304 (in thousands) as the market value of trading account assets.

b. iii.

Dr.	Securities gains and losses		
	(Statement of income)	526,197	
Cr.	Trading account assets		526,197
	To record market value of trading account assets		

c. i. Footnote A discloses that Wachovia classifies securities as held to maturity if the company has the positive intent and ability to hold the security untill it matures. This decision is made at the time the security is purchased.

c. ii. The 1999 balance sheet reports $1,048,724 (in thousands) as securities held to maturity.

c. iii. Footnote D-Securities reveals that securities held to maturity have a market value at December 31, 1999 of $1,061,150 (in thousands).

c. iv. Footnote D-Securities reveals that amortized cost of these securities is $1,048,724 (in thousands). This is the amount carried on the balance sheet. Amortized cost begins as the cost of the securities when Wachovia originally bought them. This original cost is adjusted each period untill maturity for the amortization of any premium or discount. Because held to maturity securities are, by definition, debt securities, they bear interest at a stated coupon rate. This rate may not have coincided with the market rate of interest when Wachovia purchased them and the price would have reflected either a discount (if coupon rate was less than market) or a premium (if coupon rate exceeded market). Wachovia amortizes any such premium or discount over the remaining time to maturity.

c. v. Footnote D-Securities, contains information about contractual maturity of the held to maturity securities. In banking parlance, the time categories are called 'time-buckets.' If we assume that the midpoint of each time-bucket represents the average maturity of the securities in that bucket, and select some time to maturity for the securities due after 10 years, we can estimate an overall weighted time to maturity as follows:

Time to maturity	Amortized Cost	Time Weight	Time-Weighted Amortized Cost
Less than one-year	61,131	.5	30,566
One through 5 years	534,272	2.5	1,335,680
Five through ten years	98,689	7.5	740,167
After ten years	354,632	15	5,319,480
Total	1,048,724		7,425,893

Weighted time to maturity = 7,425,893 / 1,048,724 = 7.1 years.

d. i. The 1999 balance sheet reports $7,095,790 (in thousands) as securities available for sale.

d. ii. Footnote D-Securities reveals that securities available for sale have a market value at December 31, 1999 of $7,095,790 (in thousands). The original cost of these securities is $7,214,190 (in thousands). The difference of $118,400 (in thousands) represents the unrealized losses on the securities.

d. iii. Using the same methodology as in part c, we can estimate an overall weighted time to maturity as follows:

Time to maturity	Amortized Cost	Time Weight	Time-Weighted Amortized Cost
Less than one-year	283,654	.5	141,827
One through 5 years	2,565,401	2.5	6,412,503
Five through ten years	1,314,106	7.5	9,855,795
After ten years	2,694,230	15	40,413,450
Total	6,857,391		56,824,575

Weighted time to maturity = 56,824,575 / 6,857,391 = 8.3 years. This calculation ignores the securities that have no contractual maturity. These are likely equity securities that do not mature. Consequently, the maturity calculated here underestimates the maturity of the portfolio.

d. iv.

Dr.	Accumulated comprehensive loss (Shareholders' equity)	271,010	
Cr.	Securities available for sale		271,010
	To record market value of trading account assets		

e. i. The 1999 balance sheet reports $(74,277) (in thousands) as Accumulated comprehensive loss.

e. ii. Comprehensive income is designed to capture all changes in shareholders' equity during a period other than those that arise from investments by shareholders (e.g. common stock sold by the company) or distribution to shareholders (e.g. dividends paid or treasury stock purchased by the company). Some types of revenues, expenses, gains, and losses bypass net income but are included in shareholders' equity. Unrealized gains and losses on securities available for sale are one example of how the income statement is bypassed. Items such as this are captured on the balance sheet as "Other comprehensive income" or as "Accumulated comprehensive income" on Wachovia's balance sheet.

e. iii.

	1999	1998
Securities available for sale		
Unrealized gains	19,559	141,810
Unrealized losses	(137,959)	(7,327)
Net unrealized gains (or losses)	(118,400)	134,483
Deferred taxes	44,123	(52,043)
Accumulated comprehensive income (loss)	(74,277)	82,440

e. iv. From the analysis above, it appears that during 1999, interest rates increased. Securities available for sale with fixed-coupon rates have experienced unrealized losses which implies that market interest rates have climbed above stated coupon.

f. Had securities available for sale been treated as Trading account assets and liabilities, Wachovia would have recorded the change in market value of the securities as an unrealized loss on the 1999 income statement. As the analysis in e. iii. shows, the after-tax loss is the change in the accumulated comprehensive income account 82,440 + 74,277 = 156,717. Thus, net income would have been $1,011,221 – $156,717 = $854,504. This can also be found on the statement of shareholders' equity, the last column shows comprehensive income for the year of that same amount.

g. Arguments against: Marking to market all marketable securities can introduce wild fluctuations into the income statement. Banks often hold securities for the long-term and have every intention of riding market swings out. Market values are subjective in a number of cases. Not all assets and liabilities are required to be marked to market under SFAS No. 115. This leads to a lop-sided balance sheet especially for banks that have deposits (liabilities) that are recorded at face and not market value.

Arguments for: Investors assign a value to the traded equity that reflects the true value of the firm. Market values for investment assets helps investors more accurately value firms. Wild swings in the market affect the economic value of a firm's investments. Keeping that fact off the balance sheet reduces the value of that financial statement. Investors are clever enough to understand why a firm's earnings vary widely and can adjust financial statements appropriately.

In 1998, there were significant unrealized gains in Wachovia's securities available for sale portfolio. These gains dwindled and then turned to losses in 1999 as rates increased. The CFO of Wachovia may have been reluctant to endorse total market value accounting in 1999. Although, with the relatively new comprehensive income disclosures, unrealized losses are difficult to disguise.

Teaching Notes:

The integration of a news article with a Form 10-Q SEC filing makes this case unique. Students are intrigued by the link between the financials and what the "Street" is saying. This leads nicely to a discussion of the users of financial statement information and to the role analysts play in the market.

The case points out that ratios and calculations thereof are not absolutes, they are estimates. The analysts' numbers differ from management's and students can see why by crunching the numbers themselves. Management puts a positive spin on operations which is evidenced by their lower days-to-turn numbers. The lesson is that ratios need to be carefully interpreted and the assumptions and self-serving motivations underlying them need to be known before the numbers can be accorded any credence.

Working within a seasonal industry presents analytical challenges. The income statement peaks and troughs typically lead the balance sheet by a quarter. Students have to think, in this case, about the effects of seasonality on the income statement and on the balance sheet.

Some students will fail to understand the "smooth sales" assumptions underlying quarterly ratio calculations and will report unbelievably low turnover ratios (like 1.2 times as opposed to the correct 4.8 times).

a. Accounts receivable are amounts due from customers to whom the company has made sales on account. They are sometimes referred to as "amounts due from customers," "trade receivables," "debtors" (in the U.K.) and other descriptive names.

b. Accounts receivable differ from notes receivable in that the former generally are for shorter terms and are non-interest bearing. Notes receivable are promissory notes.

c. Accounts receivable are net of an allowance for doubtful accounts and anticipated sales returns.

d. Warnaco knows that some receivables won't be collected, but at the time of the sales it doesn't know which ones. The company trades off the cost of checking individual customer's credit with the cost of not being able to collect all the receivables. The easiest way to avoid bad debts is to deal only in cash sales. This, however, will have a large impact on sales volume—an impact that normally justifies the risk of non-payment by some customers.

e. The Form 10-Q is the <u>quarterly</u> report that registered companies must file with the SEC. The Form 10-K is the <u>annual</u> report.

There are a number of differences between the financial statements included in SEC Forms 10-K and 10-Q. An important difference is the level of attestation provided by the filing companies' independent public accountants. If you refer to the Maytag case (Case 1), you'll notice that it includes an unqualified audit opinion rendered by Ernst and Young. This opinion lets the reader know that the information contained in the annual report is consistent with generally accepted accounting principles (GAAP). All Form 10-K's filed with the SEC are required to include audited annual financial statements.

Now, refer to the financial information included in the Warnaco Form 10-Q. You'll notice that the financial statements are clearly marked as "UNAUDITED." While there is no SEC rule prohibiting that audited quarterly financial information be included in the 10-Q, the cost of a full audit on this information is prohibitive. To gain a small level of assurance about the information in the quarterly financial statements, companies sometimes hire their outside auditors to perform a "review" of the 10-Q information. However, the level of assurance provided by a review is far lower than that provided by a full audit. In addition, companies might have a review performed but not publish the review report as part of the 10-Q.

Another difference is the number of periods reported in the basic financial statements. The SEC requires that three years of income statement and cash flow information and two years of balance sheet information be included in the annual reports filed with a Form 10-K (refer again to the Maytag financial statements included with Case 1). However, in Form 10-Q, companies are required to include income statement and cash flow information for the most recent quarter and the same quarter from the year earlier. Balance sheet information from the end of the most recent quarter-end and from the previous year-end is also required.

Finally, you'll notice that the footnotes accompanying the financial statements are much more abbreviated than the notes that accompany the audited annual financial statements.

f. Warnaco follows the convention in the apparel industry and prepares financial reports based on a 13 week quarter. The end of the 13 weeks may or may not coincide with the typical quarter-ends (March 31, June 30, September 30 and December 31). The most recent quarter began January 3, 1993 and ran 13 weeks to April 3, 1993. The year end financial statements comprise four 13-week quarters (364 days). As a result, the fiscal year-end is typically not the calendar year-end. Some years, reports are dated in late December and some years in early January. Every few years, the final quarter of the year is adjusted to cover 14 weeks so that the fiscal year-end does not precede December 31 by more than one week.

g.

Accounts Receivable				Allowance for Doubtful Accounts			
Beginning Balance (122,894 +2,508))	125,402					2,508	Beginning Balance
Sales (I/S)	156,750	1,000	Writeoffs	Writeoffs	1,000	1,330	Bad Debts
		139,242	Collections (plug)				
Ending Balance (139,072 + 2,838)	141,910					2,838	Ending Balance

Dr.   A/R   156,750
Cr.   Sales   156,750
To record first quarter sales

Dr.   Cash   139,242
Cr.   A/R   139,242
To record first quarter collections

Dr.   Bad Debt Expense   1,330
Cr.   Allowance for Doubtful Accounts   1,330
To record first quarter bad debt expense

Dr.   Allowance for Doubtful Accounts   1,000
Cr.   A/R   1,000
To record writeoff of uncollectible accounts

h.   Accounts receivable / Total assets
April 3, 1993   139,072 / 658,562 = 21.1%
January 2, 1993   122,894 / 629,646 = 19.5%

This increase does not fit with the seasonality of Warnaco's sales. First quarter sales are presumably lower than those in the fourth quarter of the year. The expectation would be that higher sales volume would give rise to higher proportion of accounts receivable. This is a potential red-flag.

i.   To compute the accounts receivable turnover ratio, "net sales" must be estimated for the fiscal year. A simple estimation is based on multiplying the first quarter sales by four. This assumes that sales over the subsequent three quarters will equal those of the first quarter. This may not be reasonable given the seasonality of Warnaco's business but provides a conservative approximation. (an alternative calculation leaves Sales as reported and uses the number of days in the quarter in the numerator of the Average Collection Period.

Estimate of annual sales: $156,750 * 4 = $627,000
Average accounts receivable
over the quarter: ($139,072 + $122,894) / 2 = $130,983
Accounts receivable turnover: $627,000 / $130,983 = 4.79 times
Average collection period: 365 / 4.79 = 76.2 days

j.   Average accounts receivable over the year:
                ($122,894 + $87,180) / 2 = $105,037

Accounts receivable turnover: $625,064 / $105,037 = 5.95 times

Average days held: 365 / 5.95 = 61.3 days

1993 average collection period   76.2 days

1992 average collection period   61.3 days
1991 average collection period   50.0 days

This trend suggests that the Company has increased its accounts receivable holding period by approximately 24% during the fiscal-year ended (FYE) January 2, 1993 and is projected to increase an additional 21% during the next fiscal year. This trend is not good because accounts receivable is a non-interest bearing asset. The Company could save a significant amount of interest on its revolving credit facilities if it had internally generated cash from sales. As well, as collection slows down there is a chance that the quality of the receivables is reduced.

k.   The most likely explanation is that Warnaco's management incorporated the projected growth into the estimate of 1993's annual revenues whereas the analysts performed the same simple extrapolation that was computed in part i. (above). Using the 20% growth mentioned in the fourth paragraph of the *Wall Street Journal* article, and multiplying it times FYE January 2, 1993's "net revenues," yields a projected collection period of approximately 64 days.

Estimate of annual sales: ($625,064 * 120%) = $750,077

Average accounts receivable over the quarter:
              ($139,072 + $122,894) / 2 = $130,983

Accounts receivable turnover: $750,077 / $130,983 = 5.7 times

Average days held: 365 / 5.7 = 64.0 days

Note that the other item that could have been "adjusted" (downwards) by management is the projected accounts receivable balance at the end of the current year.

A final possibility is that Warnaco has certain customers who always pay later than the others. Thus, when Warnaco calculates its average collection period it excludes sales to those customers and receivables due from them. For example, by virtue of its size, Wal-Mart may be able to convince its suppliers that they will have to accept payments every 90 days. Warnaco might not like those terms, but if they want to sell to the big discount chain, they will have to live with the terms. For analysis purposes, Warnaco may exclude its sales to and receivables from Wal-Mart.

l.   The Company had $35,000 and $3.763 million of cash at April 3, 1993 and January 2, 1993, respectively. Without referring to the attached article, there are a few items in the financial statements which explain this fluctuation. First, the "Capital Resources and Liquidity" section of MD&A notes that the first half of the year is a high production and slow sales period. During this period, the Company prepares for the selling season (fourth quarter). Without sales, a company is highly reliant on debt and equity to finance inventory production. This is confirmed by information included in the statement of cash flows. Note that operations used $23.5 million of cash while financing activities generated $24 million. The primary source of this financing was borrowings under the Company's revolving credit facilities.

The *Wall Street Journal* article raises concerns about the quality of the Company's accounts receivables. Deterioration in collections can also contribute to a reliance on outside financing to provide cash.

m.   It's hard to say whether these intercorporate comparisons are warranted. First of all, common-size financial statements would be a useful tool when comparing amounts across companies. Another important consideration is the financial statement dates of the other companies. It is apparent from the MD&A included in Warnaco's 10-Q that the Company is at the bottom of their annual business cycle. As they are in a seasonal industry, available cash could fluctuate widely. It is possible that cash balances for the other companies were extracted from financial statements prepared at different points in their respective business cycles.

n.   As stated in the *Wall Street Journal* article, a short seller is betting on a stock's decline in price over some horizon. A short seller borrows stock, sells it, and then purchases that stock at some later date (to replace the stock that was borrowed). The short seller's profit arises if the cost of replacing the shares is less that the amount received when the borrowed shares were sold. Items that point toward a decline in Warnaco's stock price include the cash-flow problems mentioned in the article.

Teaching Notes:

Learning (and teaching) the Statement of Cash Flows (SCF) is a challenge. If the Weis case is used after either Mattel or Frederick's of Hollywood the operations section should present fewer problems. Those cases prepare students for a full blown SCF by dealing with the operations section in isolation. That section seems to be most confusing for students.

Students are asked to create the entire SCF in this case. Weis's Financial Statements are sufficiently straightforward to permit this exercise. Additional information is provided as needed.

Two solutions are presented below. The first uses T-accounts. A large T-account for cash can be drawn on a side-board and entries made as students work through the problem in class. The smaller T-accounts can also be handled on side boards with the SCF on the center board. Alternatively, the SCF outline can be projected onto a screen with an overhead and updated as the Cash and other T-accounts are filled in.

The second solution uses a worksheet. Students can be given a copy of the blank worksheet (provided below) in advance so that they can come prepared to complete the SCF during class. The worksheet takes an algebraic approach which appeals to certain students more than the visual approach (the T-accounts).

Both approaches can be prefaced with the following (brief) algebraic explanation: Consider the accounting identity (A = L + E). Splitting Assets into cash and other assets we have

Cash + Other Assets = L + E.

The change in each account must, it follows, total the changes in the other accounts. Algebraically (letting Δ denote the change), this can be written:

ΔCash + ΔOther Assets = ΔL + ΔE.

Rearranging terms, we have the equation that captures the SCF:

ΔCash = ΔL + ΔE - ΔOther Assets.

The change in cash must equal the changes in liability and owners' equity accounts minus the change in all of the other assets.

Regardless of the approach taken in class, students will have different ways of creating the SCF. Many students work from the operations section down. Others prefer to deal with each balance sheet account in order regardless of which SCF section it pertains to. Calling on students to do one entry on the SCF or on the Cash T-account allows for their diversity of approaches.

Weis Markets, Inc.—Statement of Cash Flows

	Cash		
Opening Balance	4011		
Operations			
Net Income	79420	10920	Change in A/R & Prepaid Expenses (7385 +3535)
Depreciation	31504	1708	Change in Inventory
Amortization	1664	136	Change in Deferred Income Tax
Change in taxes payable	988	3395	Change in A/P, other liabilities & Min Interest*
		582	Gain on sale of PP&E
Investing			
Sale of PP&E	1107	3284	Purchase Other Assets
Sale of Marketable Securities	37428	72759	Purchase PP&E
Financing			
		34499	Dividends Paid
		25554	Purchase Treasury Stock
Closing Balance	3285		

```
*    change in AP                     -10267
     change in Accrued Expenses         4731
     change in Accrued Self-Insurance   2823
     change in Payable to EBP           -504
     change in Minority Interest        -178
```

Marketable Sec.	
453017	
16585	37428
432174	

A/R (net)	
24132	
7385	
31517	

Inventory	
130019	
1708	
131727	

Prepaid Expenses	
4229	
3535	
7764	

PP&E	
542436	
72759	2094
613101	

Acc. Dep.	
	297173
1569	31504
	327108

Intangibles & Other Assets	
29078	
3284	1664
30698	

Accounts Payable	
	82529
10267	
	72262

Accrued Expenses	
	8266
	4731
	12997

Accrued Self-Insurance	
	10462
	2823
	13285

Payable to EBP	
	7957
504	
	7453

Income Tax Payable	
	3089
	988
	4077

Deferred Taxes (all three balances)	
2344	17495
136	6770
	21785

Minority Interest	
85	
178	
263	

Common Stock	
	7380
	0
	7380

Retained Earnings	
	834995
34499	79420
	879916

Net Unrealized Gain on Marketable Secs.	
	4933
	9815
	14748

Treasury Stock	
84928	
25554	
110482	

WEIS MARKETS, INC. AND SUBSIDIARIES
CONSOLIDATED STATEMENTS OF CASH FLOWS

(dollars in thousands)
For the Fiscal Years Ended December 30, 1995,
December 31, 1994, and December 25, 1993

	1995	1994	1993
Cash flows from operating activities:			
Net income	$79,420	$76,249	$72,953
Adjustments to reconcile net income to			
net cash provided by operating activities:			
Depreciation and amortization	33,168	30,607	28,959
Gain on sale of fixed assets	(582)	(298)	(798)
Changes in operating assets and liabilities:			
Increase in inventories	(1,708)	(18,172)	(14,188)
(Increase) decrease in accounts			
receivable and prepaid expenses	(10,920)	(1,603)	3,302
Decrease in prepaid income taxes	--	--	419
Increase (decrease) in accounts			
payable, other liabilities and			
minority interest	(3,395)	28,669	11,652
Increase in income taxes payable	988	1,151	1,938
Increase (decrease) in deferred income taxes	(136)	2,769	(134)
Net cash provided by operating activities	96,835	119,372	104,103
Cash flows from investing activities:			
Purchase of property and equipment	(72,759)	(49,421)	(49,188)
Proceeds from the sale of property			
and equipment	1,107	985	1,928
(Increase) decrease in marketable securities	37,428	(15,631)	(9,448)
Increase in intangible and other assets	(3,284)	(20,058)	(7,909)
Net cash used by investing activities	(37,508)	(84,125)	(64,617)
Cash flows from financing activities:			
Proceeds from issuance of common stock	--	125	108
Dividends paid	(34,499)	(32,326)	(30,677)
Purchase of treasury stock	(25,554)	(8,101)	(1,149)
Net cash used by financing activities	(60,053)	(40,302)	(31,718)
Net increase (decrease) in cash	(726)	(5,055)	7,768
Cash at beginning of year	4,011	9,066	1,298
Cash at end of year	$ 3,285	$ 4,011	$ 9,066

Alternate Solution:

The basic premise behind preparing an indirect-method statement of cash flows (SCF) is to explain the change in the cash balance through the changes in the other balance sheet accounts.

Consider the accounting identity $(A = L + E)$. Splitting Assets into cash and other assets we have Cash + Other Assets = L + E. The change in each account must, it follows, total the changes in the other accounts. Algebraically (letting Δ denote the change), this can be written: ΔCash + ΔOther Assets = ΔL + ΔE. Rearranging terms we have the equation that captures the SCF. The change in cash must equal the changes in liability and owners' equity accounts minus the change in all of the other assets.

One way to start this process is to enter the current and prior years' balance sheet information into a spreadsheet and compute the differences in account balances. This spreadsheet also allows a way to check that every balance sheet account change has been incorporated into the SCF. Here's the spreadsheet for Weis's 1995 balance sheet:

	Beginning Balance		Transactions		Ending Balance	
	Debits	Credits	Debits	Credits	Debits	Credits
Cash & equivalents	4011				3285	
Operating						
Net income						
Investing						
Financing						
Marketable Securities	453017				432174	
Accounts receivable	24132				31517	
Inventory	130019				131727	
Prepaid Expenses	4229				7764	
Deferred Income Taxes	2344				0	
PP&E at cost	542436				613101	
Accumulated depreciation		297173				327108
Intangible & Other assets	29078				30698	
Total assets	892093				923158	
Accounts payable		82529				72262
Accrued expenses		8266				12997
Accrued self-insurance		10462				13285
Payable to emp. benefit plans		7957				7453
Income taxes payable		3089				4077
Deferred taxes		17495				21785
Minority interest	85				263	
Common stock		7380				7380
Retained earnings		834995				879916
Net unrealized gain on MS		4933				14748
Treasury Stock	84928				110482	
Total liabs. & equity		892093				923158
Total debits & credits	2166372	2166372			2284169	2284169

Weis Cash Flow Worksheet - Completed

	Beginning Balance		Transactions		Ending Balance	
	Debits	Credits	Debits	Credits	Debits	Credits
Cash & equivalents	4011				3285	
Operating						
Net income			79420			
Depreciation & Amortization			33168			
Gain on sale of fixed assets				582		
Inventories				1708		
A/R & Prepaid expenses				10920		
A/P, other liabilities & minority int.				3395		
Income taxes payable			988			
Deferred income taxes				136		
Investing						
Payments for PP&E				72759		
Proceeds from sale of PP&E			1107			
Short term investments			37428			
Purchase of other assets				3284		
Financing						
Issuance of common stock				0		
Dividends				34499		
Purchase of treasury stock				25554		
Marketable Securities	453017		16585	37428	432174	
Accounts receivable	24132		7385		31517	
Inventory	130019		1708		131727	
Prepaid Expenses	4229		3535		7764	
Deferred Income Taxes	2344			2344	0	
PP&E at cost	542436		72759	2094	613101	
Accumulated depreciation		297173	1569	31504		327108
Intangible & Other assets	29078		3284	1664	30698	
Total assets	892093				923158	
Accounts payable		82529	10267			72262
Accrued expenses		8266		4731		12997
Accrued self-insurance		10462		2823		13285
Payable to emp. benefit plans		7957	504			7453
Income taxes payable		3089		988		4077
Deferred taxes		17495	2480	6770		21785
Minority interest	85		178		263	
Common stock		7380		0		7380
Retained earnings		834995	34499	79420		879916
Net unrealized gain on MS		4933		9815		14748
Treasury Stock	84928		25554		110482	
Total liabs. & equity		892093				923158
Total debits & credits	2166372	2166372	332418	332418	2284169	2284169

Teaching Notes:

In this case, students are asked to prepare common size balance sheets for two companies (one U.S. and one Japanese) and identify major differences in their investing and financing decisions. We focus later on the debt-equity ratio and ask students to speculate why the ratios are so different. We discuss cultural factors that account for some of the difference. The next case, Fuji & Kodak also looks at the debt-equity ratio and provides a counter-example to the general trend that Japanese companies tend to have higher D-E ratios than their U.S. counterparts, due partly to the role of banks as major capital providers in Japan.

We use this case as a supplementary case at the beginning of the semester. Our goal in using the case is to help students become familiar with the contents of financial statements and to expose them to the basic inferences that can be made about companies' investing and financing decisions. Because the case focuses on *using* financial statements, the case can be used prior to teaching students how financial statements are *prepared*.

a. Yokohama Rubber Company <u>12/31/90</u>

Cash	7.6%
Marketable Securities	5.3%
Trade receivables	
Notes and Accounts	28.4%
Unconsolidated Subsidiaries	2.5%
Allowance for doubtful accounts	-0.5%
Inventories	14.3%
Deferred income taxes	0.8%
Other current assets	3.5%
Total Current Assets	61.8%
Land	5.4%
Buildings and structures	14.4%
Machinery and equipment	48.3%
Construction in progress	3.9%
Gross property, plant and equipment	72.1%
Accumulated depreciation	-41.5%
Total property, plant and equipment	30.6%
Investment securities	
Unconsolidated subsidiaries	1.3%
Other	1.0%
Long-term loans receivable	0.9%
Other investments	4.4%
Allowance for doubtful receivables	0.0%
Total investments and other assets	7.6%
Total Assets	100.0%
Bank loans	24.4%
Current maturities of long-term debt	3.2%
Trade notes and accounts receivable	20.9%
Accrued income taxes	1.4%
Accrued expenses	3.5%
Other current liabilities	5.5%
Total current liabilities	58.9%
Long-term debt	19.9%
Other long-term liabilities	1.1%
Liabilities for severance payments	2.9%
Deferred income taxes	0.5%
Minority interests	1.0%
Common stock	4.5%
Capital surplus	2.7%
Legal reserve	1.2%
Retained earnings	7.7%
Foreign currency translation adjustments	-0.5%
Total shareholders' equity	15.6%
Total liabilities and shareholders' equity	100.0%

Goodyear Tire and Rubber Company and Subsidiaries
Common Size Balance Sheet

	12/31/90
Cash and cash equivalents	2.5%
Short-term securities	0.6%
Accounts and notes receivable	16.7%
Inventories	15.0%
Prepaid expenses	2.3%
Total current assets	37.1%
Investments in affiliates	1.4%
Long-term accounts and notes receivable	3.3%
Deferred charges	4.6%
Properties and plants	53.6%
Total Assets	100.0%
Accounts payable - trade	11.0%
Accrued payroll	4.9%
Other current liabilities	3.2%
US and foreign taxes	2.8%
Notes payable to banks and overdrafts	2.8%
Current portion of long-term debt	1.0%
Total current liabilities	25.6%
Long-term debt and capital leases	36.7%
Other long-term liabilities	6.1%
Deferred income taxes	6.9%
Minority equity in subsidiaries	1.3%
Common stock	0.7%
Capital surplus	0.7%
Retained earnings	23.8%
Foreign currency translation	-1.8%
Total shareholders' equity	23.4%
Total liabilities and shareholders' equity	100.0%

A few noteworthy items on the balance sheets include:

	Yokohama	Goodyear
Cash and securities	12.9%	3.1%
Net receivables	30.4%	16.7%
Inventory	14.3%	15.0%
Property, plant and equipment	30.6%	53.6%

Both companies appear to maintain similar stocks of inventories (relative to other assets). Yokohama appears to have more money tied up in receivables than does Goodyear. As a result, Yokohama keeps more cash on hand to maintain its liquidity. Perhaps, through more aggressive collection of receivables, (if possible, given cultural differences) Yokohama could free up some cash to use elsewhere in the company. It also appears that Yokohama runs its business with lower capital outlays.

b. The total debt to equity ratios (i.e., Total Liabilities / Total Equity) for 1990 are:

Yokohama: 5.41
Goodyear: 3.27

	Yokohama	Goodyear
Total current liabilities	¥ 239,022	$ 2,293.6
Long-term Debt (Note 4)	80,897	3,286.4
Other Long-term Liabilities	4,627	550.0
Liabilities for Severance Payments (Note 2)	11,918	–
Deferred Income Taxes (Note 2)	2,057	622.9
Minority Interests	4,053	112.8
Total Liabilities	342,574	6,865.7
Total shareholders' equity	63,348	2,097.9

Yokohama's debt/equity ratio is 66% greater than Goodyear's. Before we conclude that Yokohama is a riskier company (i.e., due to the higher level of fixed costs associated with the higher proportion of debt), we need to remember that there can be important cultural and business differences across countries. When comparing ratios across domestic and foreign companies, it is important to be aware of the business environment in which the companies operate. Japanese companies tend have higher debt/equity ratios than US companies in part because of the nature of the relationship between banks (as suppliers of capital) and industry in Japan. A similar relationship exists in Germany and other continental European countries. When such close relationships exist between banks and companies, higher debt-equity ratios often imply greater confidence in the future of the company; that's why the banks are willing to provide the capital!